1

POOR FISHERMEN WITH BOATS

by

JIM SCHWARTZ

POOR FISHERMEN WITH BOATS

BY
JIM SCHWARTZ

COPYRIGHT © 1997,
BY JIM & MARTHA SCHWARTZ

CHJ Publishing
1103 West Main
Middleton, Idaho 83644

POOR FISHERMEN WITH BOATS

Drawings By: Lori Schwartz . . . . Age 22
            Julie Schwartz   20
            Wendy Schwartz   18
            James Schwartz   13
            Adam Schwartz   11

Front Cover Drawing . . . .   Lori Schwartz
Back Cover Drawing . . . .   Julie Schwartz
Editing . . . .   Karren Webb
Computerized Drawing
Layout . . . .   Jack W. Schwartz

A reprinting of this book is available at special discounts for bulk purchases, premiums, fund raisers, promotions, educational use, or for any reason that Jim feels will make him some money. He needs it.

For information contact:

Jim Schwartz
3500 Elmore Rd.
Parma, Idaho 83660
Phone # (208) 674-1012

This book is dedicated to my wife, Martha, because I had to get her permission to publish it. And, to all those mentioned in its stories.

At this time, I would like to thank all who encouraged me to have this book published. It was their constant asking of when I was going to have it done, their persistent reminding me that they would buy it, and their reassurance that lots of other people would buy it, too, that convinced me to do it. I did it to shut them up. Thanks again, because if it doesn't sell I won't feel like thanking you later.

TAILS

My Genealogy 1
Date-nut Bread 7
Apache 13
Grandpas Need Exersice Too 17
Let's Waite 'Til It Shocks Him Some More 21
Two Heads And They Kick
        You Out Of School 25
Tony 31
Piles Of Stuff 39
Cousin Joe 47
Keep The Horse, Give Me A Big Pretty Rock . . . 55
You Can Ride A Horse To Water
        But Don't Let Him Make You Drink 59
My Advanced Master Gardener 63
Old Duke 67
Tell Me Something I Already Knew 71
You're Catchin' On 75
The Hole And Rock Creek Road 81
Poor Fishermen With Boats 89
It's Not What You Say, It's Who Says It 93

TAILS

My Wife Loves Me For My Eye-O-Ta 97
Pronoun 101
Toenails 105
Stick That In Your Prop And Smoke It 109
Great Globs Of Cheese Puffs 113
Politicians Should Be Thrown Back 117
Take Me Along For The Ride 121
Jury Duty 125
I See Your Lips Move But
        I Don't Hear Any Words 129
They Don't Phone Solicit Me Anymore 131
You Are What You Eat 135
You Can Have Your Cake And Eat It To 139
Doctors Are A Waste Of Money 143
Zoie 151
The Nut Cracker My Sweet 155
Want A New Belt For Christmas?
        Burn Down Your Fort 159
I Get My Hairs Cut And Everybody's Jealous . . 163
Fur Sighted And Fuzzy Faced 167
My Way 169

INTRODUCTION

What time is it?

WHO CARES! Just be happy that you have some.

Many times I have been told: Time is money. I disagree. That's simply the interpretation of people who think they don't have enough time to get all the money they want. I understand the comparison of time to money a little differently.

Each day that I use up a little of my money I'm glad if I have some left over for tomorrow. Each day that I use up a little of my time I'm also glad to have some left over. If I go broke today, I might have a chance to make more money tomorrow, provided that I don't run out of time.

Be glad you have some time and use what you've got wisely. Write something down, publish it in a book, and sell it to everyone you can. With a little luck, long after you're dead and gone people will still be buying your book. Even though you can't take it with you. . . you could still be making money tomorrow.

Besides, nobody likes to be dead broke.

No real people were harmed during the making of this book. But, we don't want to push our luck so no guarantee is either granted or implied to anyone who reads it. All the stories in this book are true. The names are unchanged to protect the innocent. They are based on facts and actual events instead of figments of the author's imagination. However, the author reserves the right to change his mind or add additional facts in the event he decides to think of them.

POOR FISHERMEN WITH BOATS

MY GENEALOGY

 Prehistoric Man's forehead sloped backwards making his head appear pointed. He walked slouched over and he was ugly. Scientists say it's because he evolved from apes and they claim to have found fossilized remains of whom they say "Could be my Uncle Grog."

Uncle Grog had a way with women. (His way.) When he saw a woman he wanted, he hit her on the head with his club and dragged her back to his cave by her hair. Women have been messing with their hair since the beginning of time. They were always trying to keep it just right so it wouldn't slip out of a man's hand. The last thing a woman needed was for a man to loose his grip and drop her while he was climbing the cliff in front of his cave. Nothing killed the mood for

Prehistoric Man quicker than the sight of a woman splattered on the rocks below the entrance to his humble dwelling. It would make him feel like she just wasn't worth it anymore. He had gone to a lot of trouble knocking her out and dragging her this far, but now she was nothing more than dinosaur bait.

Oh well, the evening wasn't a total waste. He could kill and eat the dinosaur that would come to feed off her carcass. He would be fortunate to have so much food close to his home. Dinosaurs were bigger than most women and usually didn't have much hair which made them very hard to drag. Too bad it looked like he was going to be dining alone, though. With so much fresh meat, he would be hard pressed to eat it all before it spoiled. Even Prehistoric Man didn't like to waste food.

Man has never been known to put out much effort when it comes to catching a woman. Woman soon learned that tieing a bone in her hair for man to use like a handle was helpful and not running away very fast almost always meant he could catch her. Once caught, keeping a woman had to be easy . . . that's probably why man knocked her out in the first place.

Man found it so much easier to drag a woman with a bonehead hairstyle that he lost interest in any of them that didn't take the time to fix their hair. It was also necessary for a woman to show off her bone-do close to a man's cave. He was not about to knock her out very far away from home and drag out the dragging. Even the little cavegirls were putting bones in their hair and before long the little caveboys were chasing after them with their little clubs.

If two men wanted the same woman, they would beat each other senseless with their clubs until only one of them was left standing -- hunched over. That not only explains why Prehistoric Man walked the way he did, it's also the reason he was so darn ugly.

Humans evolved into a taller and more handsome species when they quit clubbing themselves all the time. Women who had been clubbed too many times were getting so ugly they started using an early type of mud make-up on their faces hoping to improve their looks. Just like fixing their hair, it caught on and women are still doing it to this day.

Creatures in this world have been changing since time began, and as they evolved what they used to be no longer exists today. The reason for why this happened is simple. They died.

As man became taller and better looking he also got smarter. Realizing that women also looked better if they were not beaten with a club, he started actually talking to them. Pointing at a woman, the man grunted, "UGG." Then he would point to his cave and grunt, "AHH." Translated it meant: "Want to come back to my place?" Man soon learned that if he could convince a woman to follow him home, it was a lot less work than dragging her. And, if he treated her with the respect she deserved, she might even cook him breakfast.

As millions of years passed, women became very good at talking. Most of us men, on the other hand, are still evolving. Even now, we grunt when we want

3

something. People who think they are smart call this phenomenon evolution.

I don't understand what the big fuss is all about. If our great ancestors were apes, like scientists would like us to believe, then how come there are still apes in the world today? Were apes given a choice, millions of years ago, to become either humans or remain apes? Did some apes, thinking humans were so ugly with their smashed-in heads, decide to stay the way they were and continue to eat the forbidden fruit (bananas) from the tree Adam and Eve were swinging from naked? I don't think so. I think any scientist who expects me to believe that has let too much water boil out of his beaker.

There aren't any apes swinging from my family tree. None of my naked relatives even have enough hair to look like an ape. Except for, maybe, Cousin Joe. When he gets a little older and has more gray hair, we'll be able to pass him off as a Silver Back Gorilla. Then nobody will pick on him anymore because he will be an Endangered Species.

Some of my relatives, who are old enough to have known Uncle Grog, say I look a lot like him. They say I'm short, ugly, and walk a little hunched over. I've even been known to act like him on occasion. Once, I had to club a badger to death with my shovel because it only made him mad when I ran over him with the car. I'm not going to let it worry me, though, until I start looking for my club every time my wife fixes her hair. I doubt it will become a problem.

She very rarely puts her hair up in bones anymore.

Date-Nut Bread

I was my father's favorite son when I was growing up. No matter how much trouble I got into, I was always Dad's favorite son because I didn't have any brothers. My five sisters resented how easy it was for me to be the favorite son and they united against me.

If Dad couldn't find one of his tools or something was broken, my sisters would tell Mom and Dad "Jim did it!" My three oldest sisters got me in the most trouble. Since they were bigger and faster, they could get to Mom and Dad first to tell on me. I would be putting up a good defense by answering all my parents' questions with a firm "I don't know" while my three sisters, who were pointing at me, were saying "He did it . . . we know he did!" They'd make sinister snickering snitching-sister faces at me as they anxiously awaited to see what kind of punishment they had got me into.

Mom would ask Dad, "Should we punish him now, or wait until his other two sisters get here to make it five against one?"

Believing in democracy and in a hurry to punish me, Dad said, "It's three out of five. Majority rules. We'll punish him now."

"Wait a minute," I complained. "Doesn't my vote count for anything? Maybe my younger sisters will agree with me when they get here."

"No, it doesn't count. You already said you didn't know," Dad replied.

My younger sisters always agreed with the older ones, anyway. Mom and Dad assumed I was guilty and they didn't even have witnesses. How could Mom and Dad be so positive it was my fault? They weren't home when I did it. I didn't think my sisters should be considered reliable witnesses because they were not even in the same room when the crime was committed. It was hopeless.

Most of the time, my punishment was being grounded or having some privileges taken away. I didn't learn a thing from this type of punishment. It seemed pointless since I already couldn't go anywhere or do anything. The day before, when my sisters got me in trouble, had seen to that.

Dad also dished out physical punishment at our dining room table. Mom would lure me there by saying something like "Wash your hands and come and eat." Because I was Dad's favorite son, I got to sit next to him. When we were having something I didn't like to eat and I felt that was a good reason not to eat it, Dad would thump me on the head using the knuckle of his forefinger. At the same instant I felt pain I would hear the words "Eat it!" The thump raised a bump so big on my head that from then on I was an easy target. I soon learned to eat what I didn't like. Dad compensated for this by thumping my bump and saying, "Eat faster."

I don't think Dad believed in physical punishment for girls. Once, I was quickly eating my dinner (that I didn't like) when there was a thump on my bump. "You girls hurry up and eat," Dad said. He wasn't even yelling. It wasn't fair. He never used that many words when he talked to me. Besides, if my bump got any bigger, Dad wouldn't even have to reach out to thump it.

I didn't believe in physical punishment for girls, either. Whenever I tried to dish it out, it was five against one with the odds not being in my favor.

In 1962, when I was nine years old, our whole family went on a two-week long camping trip. We hiked for a thousand miles down the middle fork of the Payette River. (That was a long time ago and much of the wilderness has now vanished. That trip wouldn't be any longer than twenty miles today.) The first morning, we had barely hiked thirty miles when Dad said it was time for a break.

Mom held up her walking stick signaling all us kids to stop. Mom had taught us to stop earlier on the trail when we tried to pass her. She had picked up a large stick and clubbed us with it. "You kids stay behind me," she said, "where it's safer."

"You don't have to use that club on us, Mom," I pleaded, realizing she was right. It *was* safer staying behind her. We didn't get clubbed with a stick.

"This is not a club. It's my walking stick."

"It looks like a club to me . . . feels like one, too," I said rubbing my bump that was now much larger than it had been after breakfast.

"It's a walking stick now and if you don't want it to turn back into a club, then do as you're told. When I hold my stick up, like this, it means for you kids to stop." She demonstrated. "And, don't run into me or I'll thump you with it."

I've always been a quick learner and I learned really quick that I don't like my bump thumped with walking sticks.

Dad decided that every thirty miles or so of hiking we should take a break. We got three breaks every day. At every break, Dad would take a can of date-nut bread from one of our back packs. Each of us kids carried about forty cans of it at the top of our pack where it was easy for him to reach.

The first time I attempted to eat date-nut bread, I began to feel sorry for my father. If date-nut bread can be tasted, eating it is impossible. A long time ago when a dentist had pulled out all Dad's teeth, it must have destroyed his taste buds. My dad could eat large slices of date-nut bread without even throwing up. It was true and this proved he was the toughest man I knew.

Fumes from the bread reminded me of running through pastures in the summer. I would trip, falling face first with my mouth open into whatever had passed from the animal that had passed by before me. Watching the long brown log of bread emerge from the can reinforced my idea of how the bread tasted.

Each of us kids had our own way to dispose of the bread while pretending we ate it. Holding it as close to our mouths as possible while rubbing crumbs off whichever side was farthest from Dad worked well. The crumbs would fall to the ground and could be mixed into the dirt with our feet as we pretended to change our sitting positions. Another way was to point up the hill and say with some excitement, "Hey, Dad, is that a deer up there?" Dad would look up the hill behind him and we'd quickly throw a big chunk of bread as far into the forest as we could. When Dad turned back around saying, "I don't see anything," we would all pretend to be chewing a large mouthful of bread.

This strategic combination of vocal and motor skills worked flawlessly for several days, but eventually Dad began showing signs of becoming suspicious. Our first clue was when he started saving himself the effort of looking up the hill. "I don't see anything," he would growl. We had to start saying things like "No, it's a bear right behind you!" or "Was that bird down the trail a little ways a grouse? I think you can sneak close enough and shoot it for dinner, if we sit here quietly eating our bread."

When one of us got caught doing what Dad called "*wasting bread*," we were forced to actually take a bite while he watched and he would smile as he waited for his victims to inflict their own punishment. The situation would then be life threatening. Jumping up, the accused would mumble "Nature calls" and hurry behind the closest tree to throwup. The hardest part was to keep from losing it before you were out of Dad's sight. Knowing how he hated to waste what he thought was food, we were afraid he'd make us eat it again. A few minutes later, after breathing was about back to normal, the victim would return saying "Thank goodness I'm still alive . . . I'm fine, except for this bad taste in my mouth."

Our family camping trip of 1962 is something I will never forget. It was the most fun I can remember ever having. The only thing that could possibly have made it any more fun would have been if we had skipped the breaks along the trail.

Hiking ninety miles a day without a break is a lot easier than eating date-nut bread.

APACHE

Apache was my first horse. Short and stocky, he was built for endurance which was a trait he found very useful while putting up with me. I never knew what breed of horse he was and he wouldn't tell me. One time, when we were alone in the mountains, he tried to feed me a line about being a Mustang. I wasn't swallowing it.

"Yeah, and I'm a real Cowboy," I told him. He didn't buy that, either.

The only time he talked to me was when we were alone. Kind of like Mr. Ed and Wilber. Some people feel you are a little nuts when you tell them you talk to horses. They think you're crazy if you tell them the

13

horses talk back. They must not have ever had a horse of their own.

Sometimes, I'd be out riding Apache and a stranger would say "He looks like a horse." Then ask, "What kind is he?"

"A Buckskin and something else," I'd answer. "But, he won't tell me. You got any idea what?"

Thinking he had never seen anybody quite like me before the stranger would say, "Don't have a clue. I've never seen anything quite like him."

"Yeah, he's one-of-a-kind all right. Worth a lot of money, too. Want to buy him?"

I always got a good laugh with that question and I never could figure out why. I really didn't want to sell my horse. I wouldn't have sold him for any amount of money. I guess the stranger already knew that because he didn't offer me any amount of money.

I was twelve years old and Apache was just a colt when my dad bought him for me. Dad left the job of breaking my new horse up to me, but was generous with a lot of good advice.

After months of hard work, I was finally able to ride him. However, convincing him to discard some of his bad habits proved to be a little more difficult. Impossible describes it better. Of course, if you were to ask Apache he would have said, "It's all Jim's fault. I learned all my bad habits from him." That's what he told me anyway.

Each time I rode Apache, he would buck for a few seconds before settling down to do whatever else he wanted. "Try to tell me he's a real Cowboy," he would think to himself. "I'll teach him a lesson."

Riding Apache was always a challenge. Clamping the bit in his teeth and trying to run away with me was a favorite game. While walking down a trail or road, he would carefully push the bit forward with his tongue. Biting on it as hard as he could, he would lunge ahead into a run. Eventually, with enough practice, I became quite skilled doing double back flip dismounts.

Once, while I was kneeling down fixing the pasture fence, Apache came up behind me. Pressing his nose between my shoulder blades, he pushed me over head first into the fence. "This is a fun game," he laughed. He continued to shove me over every time I knelt down until I slugged him on the nose. He then retaliated by biting the brim of my hat, jerking it off my head, and running to the back of the pasture. Walking up to him slowly, I would grab for the hat. He jumped back as he exhaled with a loud snort, covering my hat in horse snot before running to the other end of the pasture. Two hours of this and it was beginning to get old. Pointing my finger between his eyes I said, "Drop the hat and back away from it or I'll get my gun."

Turning his head slightly to one side and squinting evilly at me, Apache dropped the hat to the ground. Backing up slowly he said, "OK, OK, you don't have to get violent." He knew I had meant what I said. I'd pulled a gun on him several times before. (Note: Dried horse snot makes your hat stick to your head.)

My dad's horses always came to him when he whistled because they liked him. My horse did the same thing. He never told me he liked me, but he always came when I whistled. To Apache, a whistle was an invitation to torment me that could not be passed up.

Apache was bullheaded, mean, crude, and had more faults than California, but he was a good friend and the best horse I ever had. My wife likes all those traits in an animal, too, or she wouldn't have married me. She says I'm just like him.

16

Grandpas Need Exercise Too

In the late 1950's, lion hunting was good in the mountains northeast of Boise. I would leave home early in the morning intending to shoot one or two very large lions. Possibly, I would bag a new world's record trophy by shooting the largest lion anyone had ever seen. It could happen.

In fact, it did happen about once a week because I was The Great White Hunter. I always got my lion.

After returning home from a big hunt, it was necessary to tell my Grandpa Schwartz all about it. Grandpa didn't know much about lion hunting and he would listen to every detail.

Grandma and Grandpa lived across the alley from our house. A path led from the alley to the back door of their house. Halfway down the path, a large handmade bench sat in the shade of grape vines growing along one side of the path. Fruit trees of all kinds grew in the lawn on both sides of the path.

Sometimes Grandpa and I would sit on his bench while he listened to the highlights of my last lion hunting expedition. Grandpa would pick an apple from one of his trees and peel it with his pocketknife. Starting at one end of the apple, he would slowly turn it against the blade cutting a one-half inch strip of peeling. As he worked, the curly peel dangling from the apple would grow longer and longer until his knife finally reached the other end. Often, he could peel the entire apple leaving a single curly peeling that could be stretched out for three or four feet. Grandpa would cut a slice from his apple to share with me as I finished telling him about the magnificent lion I had killed with one shot.

"What kind of gun do you use for lion hunting?" Grandpa would ask, glancing toward my BB gun leaning against the bench.

"My big gun. I hunt big lions so I have to use my big gun," I said.

"You must be the world's best lion hunter," Grandpa would say. "The lions are so afraid of you, I've never seen one anywhere around here -- and I've been here a long time."

It was no wonder Grandpa was so interested in my lion hunting. He didn't know anything about lions. I never found any lions in town around our houses. I had to go up in the mountains and track down all the lions I ever shot.

18

"Grandpa, maybe sometime you should come with me when I go lion hunting."

"I'm too old to traipse up and down those mountains," he would laugh. "I get all the exercise I need sitting here listening to you."

It was getting late and turning cold out as we walked to the house. "Did I tell you I hunt bears also, Grandpa?"

"No. What kind of gun do you use for bear hunting?"

"I got a bigger gun for bears because they are bigger than lions."

"You must be the world's best bear hunter," Grandpa would say. "The bears are so afraid of you, I've never seen one anywhere around here . . . and I've been here a long time."

"The bears are way up in the mountains, Grandpa. You got to go track'em. Now pay close attention, and I'll tell you how to kill one when you find it. Good thing you got me to teach you about hunting lions and bears, right Grandpa?"

"Most exercise I've had in years," Grandpa laughed.

19

20

Let's Waite 'Til It Shocks
Him Some More

I never had any trouble catching calves when I was a kid. Staying on their backs once I got there was an accident waiting to happen.

Cowboys figure a good ride is to stay on for eight seconds. If I stayed on for eight feet I was doing well. The closest I ever got to eight seconds was after I landed on the ground and someone yelled "He EIGHT it!"

One summer while staying with my cousins, the Waites, we decided to ride one of their calves. Two of my cousins, El Jay and Dale, caught a big calf. After some discussion between themselves, they led the calf over to me.

"We decided you can ride him first because you're company," El Jay said to me while Dale nodded his approval.

"Thanks," I replied.

"Sure," Dale said. "Mom told us if you were going to stay with us for a couple of weeks, we would have to be polite. So, you can have the first turn."

I got on the calf while my cousins tried to hold him still.

"OK, let him go," I said.

The calf stood still for a few seconds and then ran straight for the electric fence. At the last moment, the calf made a 90 degree turn forgetting to take me with him. I landed head first in the fence with my arms and legs tangled in the hot wires.

The first shock came while I was laying on ground still covered with irrigation water. "I don't like this," I said to myself. I rose to my hands and knees in time for the second shock which caused me to splash back down to the ground.

It was beginning to occur to me an electric fence has a lot more ZAP to it when you're laying in water. Each time I tried to stand up, a shock would knock me back down and cause my arms and legs to flail about with spastic jerks that tangled them in the wires even more.

Between my electrocutions, I could hear El Jay and Dale laughing over by the shed where the electric fencer was plugged in. Each time I fried, a loud ZZZZTTtttt noise rattled my brain blocking out any annoying sounds coming from their direction.

22

Dale asked El Jay, "Do you think we should unplug him?"

Looking at each other, they both shook their heads and said, "Nahhh, LET'S WAITE 'TIL IT SHOCKS HIM SOME MORE."

TWO HEADS AND THEY KICK YOU OUT OF SCHOOL

The note said:

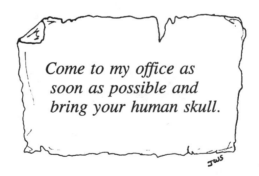

Come to my office as soon as possible and bring your human skull.

Notes from the Principal requesting me to suddenly appear in his office were common when I was in the eighth grade. Notes actually reaching me, however, was not a very common occurrence because a normal eighth grade school day for me meant I wasn't even at school.

It all started early that school year when I discovered riding my horse all day in the foothills proved to be much more exciting than a classroom.

The first time I got caught skipping school was on a Wednesday morning. The Principal called me to his office and asked me why I wasn't at school Monday and Tuesday. He knew I wasn't at home sick because his secretary had called my house to see why I had been absent so often. I then learned "The Prince" didn't like horses. He also didn't consider riding them a good enough reason not to go to school.

"You have earned yourself a truancy young man!" "The Prince" said to me. "You are suspended from school for three days and cannot make up any work you miss!"

"So what?" I thought. I wasn't going to do the work anyway. I glanced at the floor with an oh-darn-I'm-in-trouble-now look on my face. What "The Prince" didn't know was what else I was thinking. "This guy is a complete idiot. I skip school because I don't want to be there and when I get caught, my punishment is a three-day vacation. COOL!"

"We've called your mother to pick you up and take you home," he said. "I expect to see you back here next Monday. And, don't let this happen again! A second truancy and you will be suspended for *one week*."

As I left his office, I thought that the Principal was the original "Prince of Fools." It didn't take a genius to figure out that if I don't show up at school next Monday, I'll get another week of vacation. My limited education left me feeling very smart the following Tuesday when, again, I was kicked out of school.

Someone had told my Science Teacher that I had a real human skull. On one of the rare days I was actually in class, he asked me to bring it to show everyone. The day I brought it to school was the day the Principal sent the note asking me to bring it to his office.

"The Prince" was beginning to realize his form of punishment for me was not working as well as he would have liked it to, so he thought he should try a different approach. Hoping to make friends with me, the short little bald guy said, "Come in Jim, and sit down."

I walked into his office and sat down in a chair a few feet in front of his desk. I had Shine, which was my skull's name, wrapped in a white towel and stuffed in a paper bag.

"How are you doing, Jim?" he said with a smile, acting as if he was really interested. "Tell me how you found that skull."

I wasn't going to tell this man squat. I never had been very impressed with him and nothing he could say or do at this time was going to make me like him. I took Shine from the bag and rolled him out of the towel, placing him between my knees facing "The Prince." My intent was to make the shine on Shine's head match the one on "The Prince's." He didn't say a word for a long time as he watched me buff the top of Shine's head with the towel. The harder I worked, the madder he got. He was getting so angry that soon his entire head was dark red. Thinking he might explode at any moment, I worked faster. The clincher was when I spit on Shine's head and with a few quick jerks of the towel made it glow.

"That's it," he blurted out. "That has earned you another truancy."

He knew me well enough by now to know that was exactly what I wanted him to do, but by this point he would do anything just to get rid of me.

I could hear laughter coming from the secretaries in the outer office and wondered why "The Prince" had failed to see the humor in what I had worked so hard at trying to accomplish. Oh well, at least I got out of school for another week.

The other day my mom asked my youngest son, Adam, "How do you like school this year?"

"Fine," was all he said.

"Are you learning any good things?" Mom inquired.

"Yeah."

"Well, like what? Tell me what you've learned."

"School is OK . . . I guess," Adam informed her. "But I learned that work and going to school interferes with me being a kid."

I know exactly what Adam means. Any work is hard to do when you are a kid. I don't go to school anymore, but work still interferes with me being a kid. If I had tried harder in school, maybe it wouldn't be such hard work to earn a living today.

"Adam, I don't mind if you be a kid, but don't ask if you can take Shine to school. He's a trouble maker and a bad influence."

Tony

Our family moved to a small acreage west of Boise in the summer of 1966. Some kids hate to move and leave all their friends behind, but I loved our new place. Foothills to explore were a short distance away, and even closer was a drain ditch with lots of the fish in it waiting to be caught.

The next summer, a man who lived a few miles from us asked Dad if he wanted a Welch pony. "I'll *give* him to you for the kids to ride," he said. "His name is Tony and he is broke to ride and everything."

Dad and I went to see Tony at the man's place to make sure he wasn't some old swayback about ready to die with only three good legs. Although, that would have made him easy to ride. Tony turned out to be a pretty good looking horse . . . for a Welch.

The guy who wanted to give us Tony was standing next to him holding a 2x4 about three feet long. He had already caught the horse and had tied him up to a post.

Dad said, "This the horse?" as we walked up to them.

"Yeah," the man said. "Just the right size for the boy there too."

Dad looked at Tony . . . then at me . . . then to the 2x4 in the man's hand. "What's the 2x4 for?" he asked.

"Oh, just to shew off the other horses if they bother us."

I looked around the corral, but didn't see any other horses.

"Put the boy up on him and I will lead them around the corral so you can see how he acts," the man said to my Dad.

As Dad helped me on Tony the guy untied the lead rope, then holding the 2x4 in front of Tony's face he said, "Now don't you worry Tony, I won't let those other horses bother you."

Tony looked at the club and nodded like he understood the man's kind gesture. After walking the horse around the corral a few times, the man handed me the lead rope. Pointing the end of the 2x4 at Tony's head he said to me, "You ride him for a minute and see how you like him."

Tony did everything I wanted him to do using only a halter to control him. Dad and I were impressed and figured he would be a good kids' horse. Dad decided to take him.

We loaded Tony into Dad's truck. As we were pulling out of the driveway, I noticed the man was holding the 2x4 up in front of himself and spinning around in a circle. After about six spins he threw the board as far away as he could. Looking at us leaving with Tony, he put a hand on each knee and doubled over laughing. Every few seconds he would stand up, dance around, and then double up laughing whenever he seemed to look in our direction.

I told Dad, "I think that guy is very happy Tony is going to a good home."

We had just put Tony in our corral at home when a laughing neighbor walked up to us carrying a 2x4 about three feet long.

"Here, you'll need this," he said, still laughing as he handed me the club.

"What for?" I asked.

"I thought that looked like Tony in the truck when you guys drove by." After pausing to chuckle some more he said, "Hold it up towards his head every now and then when you want him to do something. He don't like getting hit in the head with a 2x4. If you act like you know how to use it, then he will be good."

"How do you know that?" I asked

"I had to use it when I had him a few years ago," he answered. "Everyone around here has been stuck with Tony at one time or another."

"What do you mean *stuck* with him?" Dad asked.

"He ain't worth nothin', and until you find somebody to give him to, you're stuck with him." Smiling as he turned to leave he said, "I gotta go call everyone and tell them the Schwartz's just got stuck with Tony. Maybe you'll get lucky and someone else new will move into the neighborhood and you can give him to them."

Having Tony was both fun and a learning experience. Tony had all the fun while I experienced learning why everyone hated him.

One day I decided to ride Tony tomorrow. You always had to decide to ride Tony a day ahead of time because it took the first day to catch him. After finally catching Tony, I tied him up short so he couldn't reach around and bite me while I saddled him. He wouldn't try to bite me if I didn't have to set my club down because it took two hands to saddle him.

The first time I swung up on him, he reached around and bit down on the toe of my boot. With a quick yank, he jerked me out of the saddle sideways. I landed on the ground with my injured foot sticking through the stirrup. Many times, on television, I had watched cowboys being drug across the ground by a runaway horse. As the cowboy bounced over rocks and was occasionally stomped on by the horse, I would think "Now that has got to hurt." I realized I was right as I limped back to the barn from the end of the pasture. It did hurt!!

On future attempts to ride Tony I learned to pay close attention while mounting up, and kick him square in the teeth as he reached around to bite my foot. A few

34

good solid kicks in the mouth and he would decide to torture me by some other means.

My wife tells me I have very ugly feet because my toes are all curled up. I tell her, "That's what happens to your toes when you kick a horse in the teeth too many times."

My cousin Joe and I were riding Tony once when Joe decided he wanted to ride to the end of the pasture and back -- alone. I handed Joe a stick and said, "You will have to hit him on the rump with this to get him to go there. But, when you start back throw the stick away."

"Why?" Joe asked.

"Because he'll bite the bit and come back at a dead run. You will need both hands to hold on."

I watched Joe beat on Tony all the way to the end of the pasture. As he turned around, Tony reared up and started running. Joe slung the stick to the side and held on for his life. I was standing by the fence laughing at Joe while they approached because I knew what was going to happen next.

A few yards before the fence, Tony dropped his head and put on the skids. Joe was thrown forward into the air, over the fence, and head first into a ditch full of water beside where I was standing. Joe was still holding onto the reins as he pulled his face out of the mud and came up for air. Tony was looking down at Joe with a smile, obviously proud of his work.

"Huh." I said. "That's the same spot in the ditch he dumped me in when I rode him to the end of the pasture."

Spitting out the mud in between calling the horse names, Joe yelled, "You knew he was going to do that?"

"Yeah, but I didn't think you would keep hold of the reins. Heck! We don't even have to catch him again like I did when it happened to me."

"Wonderful," Joe said trying to make it sound like he didn't care.

"Come on, I'll show you something he does that's fun."

We took Tony back to the corral and I got on him. "Get up here behind me now," I said. As Joe climbed on, I quickly kicked Tony in the teeth a few times. "Now kick your heels into his flanks. He's ticklish there and it makes him buck."

The more Joe kicked, the madder Tony got and the harder he tried to buck us off. Finally realizing he wasn't going to buck us off, he gave up trying completely. This, of course, spoiled our fun so we gave up also and unsaddled him. Joe told Tony we had got the best of him as he took the horse's bridle off. As Joe turned to walk away, Tony ran up behind him and bit a big chunk out of his back.

The bite bled a lot and left big black and blue bruises over half of Joe's back. I could see right away Tony did a good job and Joe could be real proud of his new wound. I don't think Joe appreciated it, though . . . until about two weeks later when it finally quit hurting enough that he could stand to wear his shirt again.

From then on, Joe did all his talking to Tony with a 2x4.

36

38

Piles of Stuff

I called my brother-in-law, Ken, to see if he wanted to go fishing.

"Hello."

"Hey, Ken, let's go fishing for a couple of days. I got a new map."

My wife doesn't like me to get new maps. It means I'm thinking of going fishing and when it's one of those topographical maps, she knows I'm going fishing somewhere way up in the mountains. My wife knows I don't like to argue so when she saw I was getting ready to go fishing, instead of trying to talk me out of it, she said, "It better be for only a couple of days. I'm eight months pregnant and your fishing trips have been known to take six or seven weeks."

I told her this trip would be two or three days, maybe a week at the most. Then, I drove to Ken's house.

We loaded our motor bikes into the back of Ken's truck and went to get our stuff. All good fishermen know if they are going fishing they have to have some stuff. Since you are going fishing it is a good idea for it to consist of fishing stuff. For an experienced fisherman, like myself, this is never a problem because I keep all my fishing stuff in a pile. Everything I would ever possibly need on a fishing trip is kept in this pile. If I don't find what I think I need in my pile, then I must not have needed it in the first place.

The experienced fisherman can never be held accountable for forgetting something so long as he had added that item to his stuff pile at least once in the past. This can always be blamed on the youngest fisherman in your group because it was his job to load up the pile. When he whines about it not being in the stuff pile to begin with, you tell him it must of been stolen and he should have told you so you could replace it. Since he was in such a hurry to load the stuff and forgot to check and make sure everything was there, now it's up to him to replace it. It's the least he could do for all the inconvenience he caused.

All fathers who take their kids fishing are automatically experienced fishermen. The father's responsibility is to tell the kids to get the fishing stuff in the truck. If anything is needed later while on the fishing trip and it is not in the stuff, it's the kids' fault.

Being novice fishermen, the kids must have forgotten it.

A friend, Bob, told me about a fishing trip he had taken with his son a couple days ago. They caught lots of little ones, but nothing they threw at the water interested any big fish.

Bob said, "Boy, a month ago I was out in my brother Rob's boat. I was using this little one-of-a-kind lure I made myself and brought in a fish every cast. Each one was bigger than the last one and the first one was the biggest of them all! Me and my boy would have done a lot better than this the other day, if I had my one-of-a-kind lure. But, Junior here, he seemed to have forgot it. I guess I can forgive him long as he don't ever let it happen again."

"Dad . . . Hey Dad!"

"What?"

"Uncle Rob said to tell you that the little one-of-a-kind lure of yours still works great. He went back to the lake last weekend and caught some even bigger fish than when you were with him."

"So that's where my lure is. You forgot to get it out of Uncle Rob's boat and put it back in the stuff pile. Remember, son, if you always put all your fishing stuff back in the stuff pile it will be there next time you need it."

"But, Dad, you didn't take me fishing with you when you went with Uncle Rob. Two days ago was my first fishing trip!"

"Don't make up excuses, son. Remember, a good fisherman never has to make up excuses."

You always want to keep all your stuff organized.

41

True outdoors men are very good organizers. We put all our fishing stuff in the fishing pile and the hunting stuff in the hunting pile. Then, whenever we want to go fishing or hunting we back the truck up to the right pile and just throw the stuff in. If you put everything away, then you waste a lot of time trying to remember where you put it.

Ken and I finished loading the stuff and headed for the mountains.

"Martha is not mad at you for going fishing while she sits at home eight months pregnant, is she?" Ken asked.

"No, she really didn't want to come along anyway. She quit riding motorcycles and climbing mountains about a month ago. Besides, we will only be gone two or three days, a week at the most. She'll be fine."

We got to the trail head, unloaded the bikes and our stuff, and started up the mountain. Five miles later, we stopped the bikes and took out our new topographical map. From here, we would have to hike because the trail had ceased to exist about ten miles back.

Topographical maps are about the easiest kind of maps to read. They tell you how high the mountains are, names of rivers and creeks, where the lakes are, and which way the trail goes. You don't want to go the way the trail goes. Topographical maps have lots of little squiggly lines on them and lots of times the trails go round and round all over the map. The lines never cross each other. As they go up a mountain peak they squiggle around until they end up right back where they started. If you follow a trail that gets stuck in between two of these lines you will never get to where you think you're going, only back to where you started.

"Hey Ken, look at this map. The trail takes off here and winds all over the whole map. Sometimes it goes a long way before crossing a line. I'm afraid we might get stuck between two of those lines and end up right back here. Look how close these lines are. There must be about two thousand of them in just a half-inch. I say we go to the right about here and we'll be to the lake in no time."

There are lots of mistakes on maps. Judging from the little scale at the bottom of the map, it was about thirty miles to the lake if we took the trail, thirty feet if we stepped over all those lines on the right. As long as they have been making topographical maps, you would think by now they would quit putting scales on them that are misleading and just write on the bottom: Area shown one square mile. Actual distances hiked may vary.

It is not unlikely, on a topographical map, to travel from point A to point B in multiple directions with all routes being the same distance. So much for the theory the shortest distance between two points is a straight line. Point A is in the middle of the map. Point B is one half-inch straight south. Four men leave point A at the same time going in four different directions. The man going south goes straight to point B. The other three wander carelessly this way and that way but, still, they arrive at point B after traveling the same number of miles. Believe me, it's true. I have gone all four of those directions, sometimes even on the same trip.

After we hiked a thirty mile half-inch, we got to the lake. It didn't matter that the map had lots of mistakes on it. Our excellent woodsman's sense of direction had gotten us there anyway.

I walked up to the edge of the water to look for signs of fish. "Hey, Ken! I wonder if there is any fish in this lake?"

Ken was looking at the fishing reel he had taken out of his pack. The line had unspinned off the reel completely, covering it in a large ball of loops and knots. The only way to fix it was to cut off all the old line and spin new line on the reel. When you put new line on, you always spin it on. How else would it get round and round that spinning thing on front of the reel? That's also why when it comes off it's called unspinned.

44

Years and years of fishing has taught Ken how to overcome these little mishaps.

"Hey, Jim! Where's that new spool of line you brought in case your reel came unspinned? By the way, see any signs of fish?"

While Ken frantically spinned new line on his reel, I started catching fish. My first nine casts had each yielded a cutthroat or a rainbow trout. On my tenth cast, I felt a fish bump my lure three times. I think I could have hooked him the fourth time he tried to take my lure if a big rock had not stopped him. He had chased my lure across the lake and had run face first into a it at the edge of the water. These fish were really hungry.

For what must of been at least two days, Ken and I were the only people at the lake. Fishing was fantastic, but I knew it was time for us to leave. "Hey Ken, I think it is about time for us to leave." I said looking around. "Ken! Hey, Ken! Where are you?"

"I'm over here."

I could see him waving to me from across the lake. "We better be leaving," I called out.

"Yeah, I know!" he yelled back. "Let's meet up on the right side of the lake."

About twenty minutes later, I walked out of the trees on the side of the lake to my right. I sat down on a rock at the edge of the water to wait for Ken. He should be there any minute. After a long time, I stood up and yelled, "Where you at?"

"Over here," I heard from across the lake.

"What are you still doing across the lake?" I asked.

"Sitting on this rock at the edge of the water, waiting for you!"

"OK. Wait there till I catch up to you," I said.

Eventually, when I finally caught up with Ken, he asked, "Which way is back to the bikes?"

"I think we came in over there across the lake. See that spot with the rock down by the edge of the water?" I turned around to check the terrain behind us just to make sure I was right. A good woodsman always pays real close attention to the terrain in the wilderness so he never gets lost.

"Ain't that the one you were sitting on a while ago?" Ken asked.

"Yeah, I think so. We better get going. If we don't waste any time, we can be back to the truck before it gets dark."

When I got home, my youngest son was seven days old. It was a real surprise since my wife was only eight months pregnant when I left about a week ago.

I always have a lot of fun going fishing with Ken and hope to go again sometime. But, I've been so busy these last few years, I can't seem to find the time.

What the heck, I'll call him anyway."

"Hello."

"Hey, Ken. Let's go fishing for a couple of days. I got a new map."

"Okay, but I hope you're not a grandpa by the time we get back!"

Cousin Joe

My cousin Joe, who lives in California, came to visit me for a couple of weeks in June of 1972. We spent his entire vacation camping and fishing in the mountains of Central Idaho.

When he got to my house we loaded our "stuff" in my pickup, a brand new 1972 red Chevy, and headed to Summit Flats. Trying to take the high road to the Flats from Pilots Peak, we found a large snow drift blocking the road.

"I guess we could shovel our way through it," Joe said. "It's only a couple hundred feet long."

"And eight feet deep! You better get started," I said encouragingly.

"What are you going to do?"

"I'll eat lunch. Besides, we only have one shovel."

Joe looked to each side of the snow drift. "Too bad it's so steep on both sides of the road and we can't drive around it."

"Yeah, too bad," I said handing him the shovel.

I sat down on a rock to eat and watched Joe work. He was digging like a mad dog, but the drift didn't seem to be getting any smaller. "You only got two weeks, Joe. Can you get to the other side by then?"

Joe looked up wiping the sweat out of his eyes with his sleeve. "Your turn," he said handing *me* the shovel.

I put the shovel back in the truck.

"Aren't we going to try and get to the Flats?" Joe asked.

"Sure, get in the truck. We'll go back and take Grime's Creek road in from the other side."

"Why didn't you tell me there was another road we could take?"

"You didn't ask me. Besides, you said we could dig our way through the snow drift. I just agreed with you. I didn't say I would do it."

"You still could have told me about the other road," Joe said a little mad.

"Yeah, I could of," I agreed laughing.

Joe wasn't laughing and he started calling me by names that were not my own. I decided maybe Joe would enjoy being laughed at tomorrow.

There were no new tire tracks in the ruts and muddy places of the road so we knew we were the first people driving into the Flats that spring. Rounding a corner, we came to a big tree that had fallen across the road.

"I guess we could chop our way through it," Joe said. "It's only about eight feet in diameter."

"And a couple hundred feet long. You better get started," I said encouragingly.

"What are you gonna do?"

"I'll find the chain. Besides, we only have one axe."

Joe looked to each side of the tree. "Too bad it's so steep and we can't drive around it."

"Yeah, too bad," I said handing him the axe.

I sat down on a rock to watch Joe work because I knew where the chain was. I had seen it in the back of the truck when I lifted the axe off it.

Joe must have still been mad about not getting to shovel his way through the snow drift because he chopped through that tree in no time. We hooked the chain to the tree and using the truck, pulled the tree sideways enough to drive around it. A short ways further down the road, we came to a bridge over the creek. Spring run-off had washed away the road on the side closest to us.

"I guess we could fill that washout up with rocks," Joe said. "It's only about eight feet deep."

"A couple hundred rocks should do it. You better get started," I said encouragingly.

"What are you gonna do?"

"I'll get the planks ready to put over the top. Besides, I wouldn't want to drop one of those rocks on you."

Joe rolled rocks from the side of the road into the washout until it was full. Then, I backed the truck up so he could slide the planks out and lay them across from the bridge to the road. We had brought the planks along to make our own bridges knowing the mountain roads would be in bad condition that early in the year. The rocks supported the planks enough to keep them from breaking in the middle under the truck's weight.

After crossing the bridge, I stopped long enough to retrieve the planks. It would embarrass me if at the next washout, after Joe had filled it with rocks, he said, "Jim, you forgot the planks." It might give him reason to call me by some other name again.

As it turned out, Joe did forget my right name again later that day. We were exploring a side road that led down a draw to an old mine. Going down a steep part of the road, we came to another large tree that had fallen across the road. When I tried to back up the hill, the tires spun in the loose gravel. As we got out of the truck, I knew what Joe was thinking so I quickly handed him the axe.

"Good thing that tree broke in two on my side of the road," I told Joe. "You will just have to chop through it on your side."

"Wonder how I knew it would be my side," Joe commented.

Surveying the situation I said to Joe, " If that tree comes loose it's going to roll right down the road, over that big washout, and crash down the hill where the road turns off to the left."

Joe had almost cut through the tree when I began to wonder how far we would have to go down the road to find a place to turn around. "Let me spell ya a minute," I said to Joe. "Why don't you go look around that bend and see how bad the road is?"

I watched Joe try to walk down the road. He would slip and fall, covering more ground sliding and rolling down the steep grade than he did on his feet. I lifted my right leg to set my foot on the tree. As I leaned forward to rest my elbow on my knee, the tree snapped apart where Joe had been chopping it.

"Hey, Joe!" I yelled.

Joe turned around to see a huge section of the tree bouncing and rolling down the road straight for him! Trying to run, he slipped and fell again. I could see an occasional arm or leg sticking up in the air above the log as Joe rolled down the road. Suddenly, Joe had disappeared. Only the log continued down the road. Looking through the dust, I could not see Joe's smashed body anywhere. Poor Joe was gone without leaving so much as a bump on the road. I was beginning to worry. If Joe was all squished flat in the middle of the road, I might not be able to drive around him to get to the turn-around spot.

Suddenly, Joe stood up. The log had blocked my view of the washout he had rolled into at the last second. He wasn't even smashed at all.

"Hey, Joe! Look at that log. It rolled off the road right where I said it would."

Joe was calling me names I had already heard several times today. As he looked at the log and then back up to me, I could see he was not near as impressed with my being right as he should be.

That night, we made camp under a big pine tree next to a creek. We were almost asleep when there was a rustling sound a short distance from our heads.

"Hear that?" Joe asked raising up on one elbow.

"What is it?"

"Don't know," Joe answered as he shined a flashlight toward the tree trunk. The only thing there was the box of crackers we had been munching on earlier. He turned the light out with a shrug and laid back down. A short time later the sound was back.

"There it is again!" I said.

Joe flipped the flashlight on, but all we saw was the cracker box.

Laying on my stomach, I took out my 357 magnum pistol and pointed it towards the box. I cocked it and said to Joe, "Next time there's that noise, don't say anything. Just shine the light on the box."

We laid still and quiet. In a few minutes the rustling sound was back, followed by a soft crunching sound. Joe flipped on the light. Sitting by the box, a mouse was chewing on a cracker about six inches in front of my gun barrel. As I pulled the trigger, the gun roared with a bright orange flash that reflected off crackers as the box exploded.

"You got him!" Joe screamed as the smoke cleared.

"Where? Where is he?" I asked

"You blew him to pieces along with the crackers!"

We looked all over between us and the tree finding lots of cracker parts, but only one small piece of mouse.

"Bet he ain't got guts enough to do that again," Joe said. "Remind me not to eat crackers after dark around you."

The next day we found the remains of an old miner's cabin that had been built with square nails. By pulling them out of the old half-rotten boards with a pair of pliers, we gathered several hundred nails of various sizes to take home.

Every couple of days Joe and I would break camp, get in the truck, and go somewhere else. We didn't have any place particular in mind to go. We just drove through the mountains and were glad to be there. If we saw a place by a creek or river where we thought the fishing might be good, then we stopped for a day or two.

Some of the things I have done over the years I enjoyed so much that I often think I would like to do them again. Camping with Cousin Joe is one of the many things worth reliving. If I ever get another new pickup, I'll call Joe and ask him if he has time to help me break it in . . . somewhere in the mountains of Idaho.

KEEP THE HORSE,
GIVE ME A BIG PRETTY
ROCK

Someone once told me the American Indians believed that before visiting another man's tepee you must give him a gift. That way he would know you came in peace and that you respected him. Unless, of course, the gift was a horse. That meant you wanted to marry his daughter. If the daughter was pretty, two or three horses would be offered . . . or at least one very big pretty horse. I didn't know if it was true or not, but I sure liked the idea. The only problem I could see with it was that I didn't want a horse.

55

After some careful pondering, it occurred to me
to let people substitute something I really needed for the
horse . . . like a rock. I need lots of rocks.
They look good in the landscaping around
the farm and I use hundreds of them for fish
habitat in my ponds. A guy can never have
too much fish habitat. It would be easy to get people to
give me rocks. Have you seen how much horses are
going for nowadays?

The next time one of my daughters' boyfriends
came to our house, I asked him where my rock was.

"What rock?" he asked.

"The rock you were supposed to give me because
you came to my house," I informed him.

"I didn't know. I don't have one," he whined.

"Anybody who comes to my house has to bring
me a rock. That way I know they come in peace and
that they respect me. Don't ever let it happen again."

"Yes, sir!" The boy said thinking I was letting
him off the hook. "I really came to see your daughter,
though. Is she home?"

"Yes, she is," I answered.

"Can I see her?" he asked.

"If you give me a rock," I said. "It better be a
nice rock, too, if it means I'm going to let you see my
daughter. Not some sleazy little one you picked up off
the side of my driveway just before you got here."

"But I don't have a rock," the boy whined again
as he slipped his hands into the pockets of his blue jeans.
"Oh, wait a minute," he said with some excitement,
feeling his loose change. "I got a dime. Will that be

good enough?"

My eyes narrowed as I looked at the boy. Kids just don't seem to have any idea what good rocks are worth nowadays. He could tell he had insulted me and he quickly lowered his head to stare at the ground by his feet.

"No, it's not good enough," I growled at him. "But, a quarter will be."

He handed me the money so fast it made me think I was letting him off too easy. I bet I could have gotten at least twice that much out of him. It left me feeling a little short-changed so I told him, "Next time bring me two rocks to make up for all the trouble you caused this time. And, they better be pretty ones if you think you stand a chance of ever taking my daughter out on a date."

I've got three daughters and I can't wait to see how many big pretty rocks I'm going to get when someone wants to marry one of them.

YOU CAN RIDE A HORSE
TO WATER BUT DON'T LET
HIM MAKE YOU DRINK

We saddled the horses and went for a ride along the canal that followed the base of the foothills. Dad was riding Brandy, a huge gelding. I was riding Pixie, another one of Dad's horses who was getting fat and could use some exercise.

I never did like Pixie, and was soon going to learn how she felt about me. We came to a wide place in the canal where the bank sloped gradually into the water. Thinking Pixie might want a drink, I rode her out to the middle where she stood knee-deep in the cold dirty water. It was late October and the flow of water to the canal had been shut off a few days ago leaving it only one-third as full as usual. "I won't even get my boots wet," I thought.

Wrong . . . Pixie decided to give me a drink. Dropping to her knees and quickly rolling on her side, she pinned my leg between her fat belly and the sand in the bottom of the canal. I yelled some names at her (none of which was Pixie) and even managed to spit out a few choice words vulgarly describing how I felt about dirty canal water.

Fighting to keep my head above the icy water as Pixie tried to roll over me, I felt a shock wave of fear that, for a moment, left me feeling even more helpless against the twelve hundred pounds of horse flesh that was trying to smash me. I had just shouted out, at the top of my lungs, whole sentences containing only swear words right in front of my father. Dad didn't stand for swearing from any of his children, so I knew I was in for it now. I might as well let the horse drown me because I was dead meat if I got out anyway.

Wide-eyed with fear, I looked up the bank towards Dad. He was wiping large tears out of his eyes with one hand (which could have been mistaken as genuine concern for my well-being) except he was laughing so hard he had to hang on to the saddle horn with the other hand to keep from falling off his horse. I looked over my shoulder to see what he was laughing at, but there was nothing there. "He couldn't be laughing at me," I thought. "This isn't funny."

Brandy stood still, watching my impending doom with a puzzled look on his face. He wasn't doing anything to help me, either, but at least he was polite enough not to laugh.

Desperately, I took one of the reins and began whipping Pixie across the face with it. It was a terrible thing to do, but this was a life and death situation. "My *life* and my *death*." From then on, I decided to become Pro-life.

As quickly as she had gone down, Pixie jumped back up to her feet. Grabbing onto a handful of her mane, I managed to stay on well enough to pull myself back into the saddle. Half frozen and feeling like I had just drank half the canal, I headed straight for home.

Dad was still laughing when we got there. He never said a word to me about my swearing and I never mentioned those words in front of him again, either. Come to think of it, maybe he hadn't heard every thing I said. I was under water most of time I was swearing. Not wanting to push it, I didn't even ask him what he thought was so *darn* funny.

You can ride a horse to water, but don't let him make you drink.

My Advanced Master Gardener

 Before we bought our farm in 1986 we lived closer to town on a small plot of ground. Although it was very small, we still had room for a large garden probably because we could not afford a house.

Every year, I learned more about how to raise a productive garden. Our meals in the summer completely consisted of things we grew. Throughout the season, my wife would can the extra produce for our winter meals. In the fall, I would gather seeds from select fruits and veggies to plant the following spring. After drying the seeds, I put them in cans to store until planting time.

My wife works very hard and is always trying to think of ways to make her work easier. She never has enough time to get everything done. Almost every day she says to me, "Will you get out there and get that

thing done? Or, do I have to do it myself? I just don't
have the time."

She had been taking gardening classes at the
County Extension Office and was becoming very wise
about plants and how to care for them. She knew of lots
more things to tell me to get out there and get done.
Several times a day she would say, "Will you get out
there and get those things done? I just don't have the
time to do it myself. I have to go to my gardening
class!"

I learn most of my gardening skills from my wife
by doing things for her. In fact, I learn almost as much
as if I were taking the gardening class with her. She
gets a lot of ideas, while in class, about things to do in
the garden and brings them all home as homework for
me.

Martha is now an Advanced Master Gardener.
She claims it's not true, but to graduate I think one of
the rules is: Don't tell other people all your good
gardening secrets. If I can't pry the information I want
out of her, I discover it by observation. I'm a very
observant gardener. I see my garden everyday. I used
to think gathering seeds in the fall was a good idea. In
the spring I would get about five acres of ground ready
to plant, then go look for my can of seeds.

"Why don't things ever stay where I put them?
There are some cans on the shelf over there, but I only
put nails in those kind of cans."

All winter long, I have observed some pumpkins
and squash placed in various spots around the
house. Slowly they sank into a rotten pool of

mold and slime. I wanted to haul them off about last Thanksgiving, but my wife said, "NO!" She wanted to keep them for their seeds.

I asked Martha, "Have you seen my seeds I saved last fall?"

"Why don't you dig up some of those new little plants growing by the house? You will find them in each one of those spots that used to be pools of mold and slime."

Observation: This is how an Advanced Master Gardener keeps track of her seeds. It is lots less work than gathering seeds in cans. Saves time, too.

I transplanted all the new little plants growing by the house into our garden and cleaned up the dried up mold and slime. Martha said, "It looks very nice."

"Thank you," I responded. My wife always compliments me on my good work so the least I can do is be polite.

"By the way, Jim, your seeds from last year are on the shelf in those cans you only put nails in. Remember? They were the only cans you found last fall and you said you would put them in the right cans, later . . . when you found them."

"Thank you."

"Oh yeah, your seed cans are in the shed with bolts in them. You might want to put the bolts in the bolt cans and get your seed cans ready for this fall."

"Thanks, I'll do it later."

The guy on the other end of this line said if I don't
hold my mouth right you won't bite.

Old Duke

Duke was ten years old when we bought him from a man in Boise five years ago. My wife and kids liked him well enough at first. But, now they don't want to be seen associating with him. They claim he's dirty, old, and decrepit . . . just like me. I'm told things like "We can't even touch him without getting filthy," and "Why don't you ever wash him?"

"Hey, he stays outside and gets washed off whenever it rains," I say.

Last month the whole family took Duke for a run around the farm. We all had fun while he crashed through the corn field and ran all over our foothills. Sometimes he would sail through the air when he jumped off the bank at the side of our road and then he'd land in the field below.

I don't take Duke very far away from home anymore because I'm afraid he won't make it back. He's only good for two or three miles before he starts coughing and sputtering and going into fits of jerky convulsions. He acts like he could crap out any second, but so far he has always managed to keep going until we make it home.

In the spring I take Duke gopher trapping up the draw behind our farm. He'll run full speed, splashing through big muddy pools of water in all the low places of the road. By the time we get to a field with gophers, Duke needs a rest so he waits by the edge of the field while I set traps. After an hour or two, he's cooled down enough to make it back home. When he was younger I would take him from gopher mound to gopher mound all over the field with me, but now it's just too much for him.

Some of my friends will bring their dogs out during pheasant hunting season and we will all take Duke to the fields looking for birds. This puts a lot of wear and tear on Duke and I don't think he'll survive another season. When he dies, I'll park Duke next to an old blue suburban that died a few years ago and transplant any of his vital organs that still work in the next farm car I get.

Old Duke might be dead and gone someday, but this way a part of him will live on forever at our farm.

TELL ME SOMETHING I ALREADY KNEW

The other day my wife asked me, "Why don't you write about something funny?"

"I tried that once," I told her. "But, people laughed a lot."

"Then let me read it sometime. I like to read funny stuff."

"I can't," I said. "I threw it away."

"Why?" she barked getting irritated. I don't know why she insists on talking to me if it irritates her so much.

"Turns out they were laughing at me instead of my story," I said. Most people act like I don't have any sense at all, let alone a sense of humor.

I never make anything up to write about because I don't write fiction. My wife gets mad at me if I make stories up. I used to make them up all the time because I thought if I told her the truth she'd get mad. That didn't work, so I tried the truth about what I did and she got mad anyway. If it would make her happy, I'm willing to tell her exactly what she wants to hear. I'll do it, too, just as soon as she tells me exactly what that is.

Never being the type to want to do anything half way, I came up with an idea I was sure would work. I'll simply forget about doing all those things that make her mad in the first place. That didn't work, either. Now she makes up reasons to get mad at me and says it's because of something I forgot to do.

"No way," I said. "I forgot to do those things on purpose because when I did them you got mad at me. Now if I don't do them any more, you still get mad because I forgot how to do them. This isn't fair."

"If you weren't so stupid you'd understand," she replied.

"Don't try to use that as an excuse for being mad," I told her. "I know my doing stupid things makes you mad, and that's why I make sure those are the things I forgot how to do." She should be a fiction writer. She's good at making things up.

I've noticed lately my wife's memory is not as good as it used to be. She will read one of my stories and say, "That isn't the way I remember it happening."

"How would you know?" I asked. "You weren't even there."

"Yes, but you've been telling that story for years and it changes every time you tell it."

"I just remember a little more each time. They say if you tell a story over and over enough times it will get so good that people will think they were actually there."

"You better keep practicing because I still know I wasn't there," she said.

"Yeah, I remember. That's why *I'm* telling the story."

Starting to sound irritated again she informed me, "Maybe there is some truth to the old saying that the memory is the first thing to go."

"No, it isn't," I argued thinking I had lost something else. "But, I don't remember what I lost first. I wonder if I still need it?"

"You didn't need it when you still had it, or you would have used it more often," she said with some hostility.

"I wonder if I miss it?" I asked a little curious.

"I know I don't," she answered. "And, don't ask me to help you find it because I'm still mad at you."

I don't know why I have to start remembering to do what I forgot to do since I don't do those things any more because I forgot how to do them. Anyway, she doesn't miss what I don't remember how to do and I don't know if I ever knew how to do them in the first place, so it isn't my fault.

Sometimes when I talk to my wife, I can't figure out what we are talking about. She knows, though, and that's good enough. No sense in making things complicated.

74

YOU'RE CATCHIN' ON

I told him the same thing I tell everyone who asks me to take them fishing for their first time. "In order to be sure you are going to catch fish, first you must think like a fish."

"How do I do that?" he asks.

"Pay attention to me and do what I do. It comes naturally to good fishermen like myself. When a fisherman is good at fishing, he knows it. Just ask one. He'll say, "You're darn right I'm good. Been fishin' all my life. If there's anything I do good, it's fishin'." It's true, too, because fishermen don't lie. In fact, some of us fish so much it's the only thing we are good at."

"I'll grab my pole and bait it up," he says.

"I hope you're not another one of those guys who thinks baiting a pole and throwing it out in the river catches fish. Beginners lose more poles that way. I'll keep this simple cuz thinkin' like a fish requires a lot of brain cells to be working at once. You did bring enough brain cells, didn't you?"

I hate it when people borrow my brain cells. It's bad enough when they borrow my fishin' tackle.

"Hey, I'm not stupid: I meant I'd bait my hook and cast it out. What size hook do I use?"

"I like to use a 2/0 or 3/0 for catfish," I said.

"Ok, can I borrow one? All I have is size 8."

I handed him a hook and picked a 3 ounce sinker out of my tackle box. He tied the hook on and pulled some small split shot sinkers out of his pocket.

"How many of these should I use?"

"About a hundred," I said. And I handed him the sinker I'd been holding.

"Wow, that's heavy. How's a fish even gonna drag that thing around?"

"We ain't fishin' for minnows here. Besides, there's a lot of current out there. You catch one of the big ones and he won't have any trouble with that sinker. You'll be lucky if he don't drag you in. I wouldn't worry too much about it, though."

"Why not?"

"Because if anybody is going to catch a big one, it will be me."

After a couple hours of fishin' my friend asked, "How come you're catching all the fish and I can't even get a bite?"

"I told you I was a good fisherman."

"I'm doing everything the same as you, unless

there's something you're not telling me."

"There is one thing I didn't tell you," I said. "I'm a good fisherman and you're not."

"Ok, so you're a good fisherman. Now, tell me why I'm not catching anything," he growled.

"You're not holding your mouth right," I replied. "No matter what else you do, you gotta hold your mouth right to catch fish."

"Bull!" he barked. "I don't believe that."

"You got any other idea what it could be?" I asked.

"Well, no. Isn't that just something fishermen say?"

"There you go. That proves it. Remember, fishermen don't lie. I first heard about the trick from my dad years ago and he learned it from his dad. All good fishermen tell others about this trick."

Sounding less doubtful he asked, "Do you really think it works?"

"Sure I do. It will work just as good for you now as it did for me when I first heard about it. But, it's not something that anybody can teach you. You have to keep practicing fishing until holding your mouth right just comes naturally."

"How will I know when I'm holding it right?"

"That's easy, you'll start catching fish. Another thing my dad says to do is if people ask you where you caught a fish, hook your finger in the side of your mouth, pull it sideways and say, 'right here.' Doesn't make them laugh, but they look at you funny. Oh yeah, and if they ask how big it was, Dad says to hold your

thumb and forefinger as far apart as you can
and say, 'this big.' They'll say something like
'so what' or 'big deal.' You say, 'Yeah, this
big . . . between the eyes.' Gets'em every
time."

"If they weren't really that big, though, I'd be
lying."

"No way. Just lay a couple of 'em on the ground
far enough apart you can touch their eyes with your
thumb and finger. Then you can say their eyes were that
far apart without lying. A good fisherman can always
see to it he doesn't have to lie."

"But, what if I don't catch any fish . . . like
today?"

"Then you can say, 'I didn't feel like cleaning any
fish today, so I didn't keep any.' No fisherman ever
feels like cleaning fish so that's not a lie, and they don't
have to know you didn't keep any because you didn't
catch any."

"Ah, but what if they ask how big the ones were
I didn't keep?"

"It's good you're asking all these questions. You
need to have the answers planned out ahead of time so
it doesn't look like you're trying to think of them when
someone asks. You see, it's important to always think
like a fisherman, too, and be prepared. Besides, you
don't want anyone to know you were too dumb to think
like a fish. Just tell'em, 'Well, I didn't measure any of
them,' (because you didn't), 'but, they could of been
about this long,' and hold your hands as far apart as you
think you can get away with without anybody thinking

78

you might be stretching it. They could have been, too, if you could of caught them."

"Is that why fishermen rarely actually have a big fish to show their friends and just stories to tell?" he asked.

"You may not be catchin' fish today, but you're catchin' on."

The Hole and Rock Creek Road

A few years ago I took my friend, Chuck, fishing. At the time, I was working for a construction company in Boise framing houses. Chuck was a new guy on the crew. At lunch time I would tell the guys stories about my fishing trips. From the things I would tell them, Chuck got the impression that I must be about the world's best fisherman and I caught lots of fish . . . really big fish. Chuck's impression was right, too. Like all good fishermen, I never tell a lie.

One morning Chuck and I left to go fishing on the Owyhee River in Southeast Oregon. "We will be catching mostly Channel Cat," I told Chuck. It was a three hour drive to the river so I knew I had plenty of time to explain to him how to catch lots of fish.

Chuck must have also realized this because he asked, "How do you fish for Channel Cat?"

Very quickly I told him, "When I get to the river I take out my fishing pole, bait up the hook and start catching lots of Channel Cats." The educational part of the trip over, we could now enjoy the rest of the drive.

At the edge of the canyon, we turned down Rock Creek Road which starts as a small crevice at the top of the canyon wall. It's called Rock Creek Road because the creek is nothing but rocks and the road is on top of the rocks. The rocks are small at first, which is not good because it makes the road small also. As I followed the creek down the rocks got bigger, and of course, so did the road. By the time I reached the bottom, it was a four-lane freeway with rocks as big as semi-trucks. Just like trucks on the freeway, those rocks didn't get out of my way. I weaved the car back and forth on the creek bottom, occasionally bouncing off the bigger rocks, until we reached the river.

Rock Creek only runs water when thunderstorms are severe enough to make it flash flood. I have never seen any water flowing in between Rock Creek and the road. I've never talked to anyone else who has seen it, either. Probably because if they were on Rock Creek Road when Rock Creek was flash flooding, they are somewhere downstream in Owyhee Reservoir and in no mood to talk about it.

We had fished most of the day at Rock Creek when Chuck said, "Boy, I'm catching lots of fish. This is more than I've ever caught in my life."

I was doing pretty good myself, having already caught at least twice as many fish as Chuck had, but I didn't rub it in. Besides, who was counting? It's not like fishermen ever keep score. When you are one of the world's best fishermen, you don't have to rub it in. Everybody already knows how good you are because of the stories you have told them several times in the past.

"Hey, Chuck! I know a spot up the river where the fishing is even better than here. Of course, we will have to drive back up the creek and follow the canyon wall for a ways until we find the road. We can make it before dark, though."

We bounced off the same rocks driving out that we bounced off driving in because they hadn't moved out of the way. After reaching the top of the canyon wall, we followed the edge of it for about ten miles.

This part of the canyon was very narrow with high cliffs on both sides. A fence ran along the edge of the cliff and eventually we came to a gate. A sign on the fence post read:

Chuck asked, "Why does someone want a gate kept closed out here in the desert? There are thousands of square miles out here with no fences, except right here by the cliff. What are they trying to keep out?"

"They're not trying to keep anything out," I explained. "They're trying to keep the cows in. If one decided to fall down that road on the other side of that gate it wouldn't be anything more than a cow pile by the time it hit bottom. Cow piles, cow pies, cow chips . . . it don't matter what you call it. Out here on the desert a cow pile ain't worth nothing."

We got out of the car and opened the gate. Walking to the edge, Chuck commented with some concern, "This road is really steep."

I told him reassuringly, "It's not that bad. See those little spots down there?"

"Down there where the road sort of slopes toward the river?"

"Yeah. Those used to be cows before someone left the gate open and they got out. Now they're just cow piles. After we fall down that far, we bounce off some of those rocks and maybe two or three of those cow piles, and then coast on down to the river."

Not wanting to make Chuck worry for no reason, I didn't explain to him that we coasted down to the river because it was still so steep that first gear wouldn't hold us back. You should never let minor obstacles that get in the way bother you when you're going fishing. It's best to just bounce off them and keep going. The important thing is to get to the fishing hole. Experienced fishermen like myself let someone else worry about how we are going to get back home.

As we got back into the car Chuck said, "You would have to be out your mind to go down there!"

"My wife always tells me I've got to be out of my mind." I stepped on the gas and the car jumped over the edge into what is called "The Hole."

When the car bounced off of a couple of cow piles that softened our landing, something grey and hairy flew by Chuck's head and ricocheted off the windshield. "What was that?" Chuck yelled as he ducked down almost under the seat. "Did you see it?"

The grey hairball had clawed its way across the dashboard and tried to jump over me into the back seat. It would have made it, too, if my face hadn't got in the way. "I see it now," I said as I tried to pry it's claws out of the back of my head.

"Look out for that big rock!" Chuck screamed.

We slammed into the rock so hard it smashed the hairball between my face and the steering wheel. This helped loosen the creature's claws from the back of my head allowing me to throw the hairball to the rear of the car. I said to Chuck, "Oh, it's just another one of the kids' cats. It will ricochet off each one of the windows, for a while, trying to get out. Next time it comes at you, open the door so it can jump out."

"Whoa, did you see the way he bounced off that big rock?" Chuck laughed. "That had to hurt!"

"The kids loose more cats that way. I get home after a fishing trip and somehow a cat ends up in my car. It's looking for fish, I guess. Anyway, if it's still in the car when I go fishing again, it's too scared to come out from under the seat. Sooner or later, I hit a big bump that knocks it out from under there and, well, you know the rest."

By this time, we were coasting down to the river. I always knew how fast I was going while coasting even though the speedometer didn't work. My speed was always the same as the RPMS. Twenty-five hundred RPMS means about twenty-five hundred miles an hour. Being off by a little bit one way or the other didn't seem to matter much at that speed anyway. On the corners it's best to keep the wheels in the ruts because they help hold the car on the road. Usually, there is more than one rut to choose from and it can be confusing to the inexperienced driver. This need not be. Always put the wheels into the deepest rut. It will hold you back better. If the bottom of the car drags it will just help slow you down. Driving between two large rocks that are a little too close together for the car to fit helps, also. Besides, there ain't no sense in wastin' the brakes and good fishin' time because you don't need to stop until just before you reach the river anyway.

Upon stopping, just before we reached the river and as I was getting out of the car, I said to Chuck, "You stay here and worry about how we're going to get out of here.

By the time you get it figured out, I will have caught plenty of fish for both of us."

When he didn't answer, I looked over to the passenger's side of the car and saw Chuck was already gone. Glancing around, I could see him kneeling next to a tree with his hands folded in front of him and his head bowed down.

"Hey, Chuck! I know you're really glad I brought you fishing with me, but just a simple thanks would be good enough."

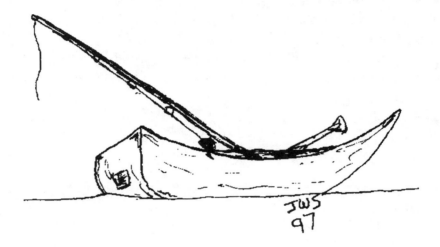

Poor Fishermen With Boats

We stopped the car by the gas pump and got out. My friend Chuck said, "Look at all those nice boats. Bet you wish you could afford a boat like one of them."

"I could afford one if I didn't feed my kids for about a year. Do you think they know how much I sacrifice for them?"

A big fancy four-wheel drive pickup pulled up on the other side of the gas pump. Behind it was a big fancy trailer with an even bigger and fancier open bass boat on top of it. A man got out of the truck wearing a designer vest and cap. He had big expensive lures hooked all over the front of his vest and everywhere on his cap.

"His type don't care about catching fish, he just wants his stuff to be bigger and fancier than everybody else's," I told Chuck.

Before the guy could fill the 250-gallon gas tank in his boat I said to him, "Sure a lot of boats headed to the reservoir today. Some kind of tournament going on?"

"Yeah. A big bass tournament," the man said.

"Me and Chuck here are headed up there, too. Maybe we'll see you there."

"Coming up to watch the tournament?" he questioned.

"No, we are going fishing up where the river comes in. We'll be on the bank, though, because we don't have a boat."

"Oh!" he said, with his nose a little higher in the air. "Can't afford one, huh?"

I got back in the car a little peeved, and drove off towards the upper end of Owyhee Reservoir.

"Don't let that guy get to you. We'll catch more fish than he will anyway," Chuck said.

"He ain't gettin' to me. I just wish I had a boat. I'd enter that tournament and beat the pants off that guy."

"What makes you so sure?" Chuck asked with a puzzled look on his face.

"I'd tie a rope around that *bass-turd* and troll with him. With all that fancy hardware hanging off him, I would probably snag every fish in the lake."

"That would do it all right," Chuck agreed. "I wonder if he knows how lucky he is you feed your kids."

"If I got him hung up on the bottom I would cut the line, too. I mean . . . what the heck. I really wouldn't be out anything. I didn't have to pay for all that fancy stuff."

When we got to our fishing spot, big black clouds were coming over the mountains to the west of us. Soon, everything across the reservoir turned white in the worst hailstorm I had ever seen. It was almost to us when a strong wind picked up forcing the storm downstream over the water. Fishermen in boats were frantically trying to make it to shore. We sat on a grassy bank in the warm sunshine while poor fishermen with boats shivered, wet and cold, in the driving hailstorm.

I will never trade my five kids to be a poor fisherman with a boat.

IT'S NOT WHAT YOU SAY,
IT'S WHO SAYS IT

It was lunch time when Dad and I finished stacking a truck load of hay in his barn. "Well," Dad said. "We better have something to eat."

"Ok," I said quickly. You don't *think* about eating at Dad's house. He does that for you. Dad decides when, what, and how much you are going to eat. Twice as much as you thought you wanted if he would have let you think about it. He makes it so easy all you have to do is figure out if you're hungry, or not. Dad doesn't concern himself with that because it's not important. According to him, when it's time to eat, you eat. If you're not hungry, then you should be unless there is something wrong with you.

I find it saves time to just eat instead of trying to explain to Dad what's wrong with me.

As Dad and I were walking to the house, we saw my step-mother, Janell, and sister, Debi, looking for us.

"You're just in time for lunch," Dad said to Debi. "We're having hamburgers."

"Oh, that's OK. I don't eat meat anymore," Debi answered.

I looked at Debi and asked, "What do you mean you don't eat meat?"

"I mean, I don't eat things that used to be alive anymore," she said.

"Well, it's not alive anymore so why not eat it?"

"No, smart @*#! I eat vegetables and stuff like that now," she scolded.

"That stuff comes from plants," I said. "They are alive when you walk up and tear a part off of them and eat it raw."

Then I contemplated to myself. How would she like to be a plant sticking out of the garden, just minding her own business, while people ripped off parts of her body and stuffed them into their mouths? Debi, the poor helpless little plant, would be stuck there watching her own juices drip off the chin of her attacker.

Can you imagine anyone barbaric enough to treat a cow like that? Pick off a piece of her while she's standing in the pasture minding her own business and then eat it right in front of her with the blood dripping down their chin. I would never treat a cow like that. It would be too much to look into those tear-filled big brown eyes and swallow raw meat. It's better to kill her and throw the eyes away. Besides, if enough people become vegetarians, I can eat the whole cow myself.

My thoughts were interrupted when Janell said to Dad, "She doesn't have to eat it if she doesn't want to."

I've been told it's not what you say, but how you say it. Dad shrugged his shoulders and went to get the hamburger. He never let it go that easy when I was a kid and said I didn't want to eat something. First, he would give me a couple of knuckle bumps on top the head and then tell me to EAT IT! You learn not to voice your opinion unnecessarily when you have knuckle bumps surgically removed from your head. I've also learned it's not what you say, it's if Janell says it.

My kids say when Grandpa gives them twice as much as they think they want, he makes them sit at the table until they're ready to eat it. I'm sure it wouldn't matter to him if they sat there until the next morning and ate it for breakfast. However, before long, Grandma would come along and say, "Oh Jack, they don't have to eat it if they don't want to." I bet they would get some knuckle bumps if Grandma wasn't there when they got up to leave the table.

Dad put one of the hamburgers he burned on his gas grill on my plate. Chipping off a piece with my fork, I noticed it was only light black in the middle.

"You won't find any E-coli's in that!" Dad said, looking at my hamburger. "That's why I cook'em like that."

I found it crunchy, but surprisingly good when I tasted it.

"How is it?" Dad asked.

It was a loaded question and I hadn't seen it coming. "Good," I mumbled between crunches, not even having to lie.

"Then you better have a couple more," Dad said, slapping two hamburgers down on top the one I was chiseling on.

Janell looked at me. "We buy it on sale," she said, "in a ten-pound package. If you buy one that big, you get another one free."

"So, how come I only get three hamburgers then?" I complained.

"Here, you'd better have some of *these*," Dad said as he shoveled twice as many pickled beets on my plate as I thought I needed.

My Wife Loves Me For
My Eye-O-Ta

When I was a boy I was a lot smaller than I am now. Other than that, my wife says I haven't changed one eye-o-ta. I don't even know what an eye-o-ta is, let alone how to change one.

When I asked her what an eye-o-ta was, she gave me *THE LOOK*. All husbands know what *THE LOOK* is. Wives don't have to say a word. Their eyes say it all. You look at them and know right away they're thinking "You're Stupid."

I've been using the same two or three eye-o-ta's for 42 years and they've been doing just fine. I haven't changed one yet, and I'm not going to try to learn how to now.

If I'm the same now as when I was a boy, then I'm using the same eye-o-ta I was using when she married me. She loved me for my eye-o-ta then, so she must love me even more now. Because if anything, my eye-o-ta has gotten bigger.

Why do wives always try to make their husbands change just one eye-o-ta? You never want to give in and change one because if you do a woman thinks "Ha, I got him now." She won't stop until she's forced you to change every single eye-o-ta you've got.

I tell my wife I can't change one eye-o-ta because she won't tell me which one has a problem. She gives me *THE LOOK* again and I know what she's thinking.

The problem with women is a hormone thing. They all have it. It doesn't happen on any particular day or at any particular age. It happens exactly 3 days after they marry you. You're just sitting there, minding your own eye-o-tas, when this hormone explodes in your wife. For the rest of your life, she will be possessed to change you.

My wife is wrong if she thinks I'm stupid because just the other day I had a really smart idea and a guy can't have any of those if he's stupid. My idea was to make a video that would show people the importance of wearing a seat belt.

I stood on top of the car while my wife drove it about 40 mph through our corn field. At the end of the field she slammed on the breaks. I flew off the top of the car onto the hood and crashed to the ground. This would not have happened if I had been wearing my seat belt. It's not important that I did not have a seat on top of the car to belt myself into, so don't think about that.

My wife told me it was a stupid idea. I could see it in her eyes. But, I think she was just being modest and letting me take all the credit for a smart idea. I mean after all, she was the one driving the car. She wouldn't have done that if she hadn't liked the idea . . . would she?

I told her that I knew she agreed with me, and to this day, she still won't admit it. Every time I talk to her I get *THE LOOK*.

I do not understand how, in 40 years, that woman has kept from changing one eye-o-ta.

Eye-O-Ta
Love Ya
For The Rest
Of
My Life

Pro-noun

My daughter, Lori, was reading some of my writing. For no apparent reason she asked, "At anytime, Dad, did you know what a pro-noun was?"

I told her, "Of course I did . . . at one time. I'm just not quite sure what time it was when I knew. Probably 3:00 p.m. on a Monday."

I can't seem to remember what those pro-nouns stand for. Sure thing, though, if they are a good cause then I'm for'em. My daughter says pro-nouns are pretty important. She's pretty smart and knows about lots of things and what they stand for.

I asked her if she thought I was important, too. She said, "Of course you are, Dad."

101

"Well, if I'm important, then maybe I'm also pro-noun."

She said, "Sure Dad, whatever."

I hear that a lot. I'll be talking to somebody, somewhere, sometime. I'm not quite sure exactly what time because I never carry a watch. Anyway, I'll be talking to someone and every so often they will slip in a "Sure, whatever." Almost everyone I talk to will say "Sure, whatever" every minute or so. It is almost like they have all been pro-grammed to say the same thing every sixty seconds. I read somewhere it's because of this high-tech ciber-space computer world we live in nowadays.

People are actually being pro-grammed to act alike. I think it's because people are not as confident in themselves as they used to be. They need to feel more important. When I ask them if they want my advice, they say "Sure, whatever." And I'll say, "Hey, why don't you just go pro-noun? If you are pro-noun, then you can feel important." Pro-noun must be one of those good things. Some people could learn a lot if they would just be a little more pro-noun. It's sure helped me.

I'm also pro-choice. I don't do anything unless it's my choice. I'm very independent that way. Years ago I used to be pro-create, but I'm getting too old for that now and had to give it up for pro-duce. My wife was also pro-create, but had to give it up for the same reason and she wishes I wouldn't pro-ceed with this. Now every spring, we both re-pro-duce. But, only when we re-plant our garden.

When we were both pro-creators, we never had any money. It's expensive to be pro-create and can make you become pro-lific. The first few years were tough, but since we've both gone pro-duce and we both work darn hard at it, too, we are finally starting to show a pro-fit.

Some people call me a pro-casterator. It's true. I believe in it for bulls and some other animals, but it's never gonna happen to me just because I gave up pro-creating.

My wife says I'm pro-verted and if anyone would know that for sure it would be her. I told her I was pro-gun and she said that was only one of my pro-blems.

Fishing is my favorite pastime, so I've always been pro-bait. I used to go fishing all the time, but my wife put me on pro-bation and that led to me taking up pro-fanity.

My kids are all pro-digies, but that's OK. My wife says it's not my fault.

Sure, whatever.

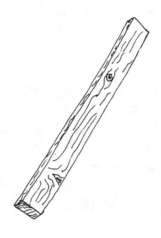

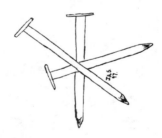

TOENAILS

His first day on the job he got there early and was waiting for me to show up. He was talking to a couple of his friends who also worked on the framing crew, and had helped him get the job by putting in a good word for him. They knew just the right thing to say. "He's a good man and will work hard. We think he's worth you giving him a try." If they had said anything else, I would have figured it was 'BULL'.

I got out of my truck and yelled at the guys because my sawhorses weren't set up and nobody was ready to go to work. They knew we were setting Carl up for initiation, but he didn't.

"OH, CRAP!" one of them said. "Hurry and get

busy. Jim gets mad and then he yells at us all day long. He'll make us work ten times as hard and quitting time won't be until it's too dark to see . . . if we're lucky."

Carl looked worried, but tried to act busy even though he didn't know what to do. Our plan was working out great.

Aiming my finger at him I yelled, "CARL, COME HERE!" and pointed to the ground in front of me. Carl ran over and stood right where I was pointing.

"Hi, I'm Carl," he said. "I really need this job and I'm glad you hired me."

"I know who you are," I growled. "I called you over here didn't I?"

Carl looked to the ground. He might as well have said "Yes, I'm afraid of you just like all the new guys. Now what?"

"I'm going to tell you the same thing I tell everyone on their first day. There's three ways to frame a house, the right way, the wrong way, and my way. We do things my way or I fire you. You got until noon to show me what you're worth and make me like you or you're fired. Now, go to work!"

"What do you want me to do?" he asked quietly.

"Go up on the roof and help the guys there," I snarled at him. "They'll tell you what you need to do and you'll be out of my face. If you can make it through the day, consider yourself hired."

Carl was so scared of me he was shaking as he climbed on the roof, but I was confident the guys would make sure he didn't vibrate to close to the edge and fall off. What Carl didn't realize is that he was about to take

106

his first and most important test. He needed not only to be capable of doing the work, he had to get along well with the crew. I trusted the guys' judgement. They would tell me what they thought of him, later.

In a couple of hours, Carl walked by me with a puzzled look on his face. I didn't know what was going on, but knowing my crew as well as I did guessed they were putting him up to something that would make him look stupid. We were always playing tricks on each other. A new man was easy prey. He entered the trailer we kept our tools and supplies in, and after rummaging around for a while yelled back to the guys on the roof, "I can't find them!"

"Can't find what?" I asked.

"We got to toenail that end truss down and I can't find the toenails," he complained.

Smiling I said, "Walk to the back of the trailer."

"Ok? I still don't see them."

"Now, look straight down."

"Ok," Carl said again.

"Do you see them?" I asked.

"Noooo," came a slow answer.

"Then take off your shoes and you'll see'em.

Carl stepped out of the trailer red-faced with embarrassment. "I'll get even with them," he muttered as he climbed back on the roof, "as soon as I think of something." It wasn't noon yet, but I could tell Carl was going to work out just fine.

After work we all joked with Carl about giving him such a bad time. He even told one of the guys, "Maybe Jim's not such a bad boss after all."

One of the guys, who planned to quit anyway, laughed in disagreement. "Wait until you get to know him."

"Hey, slime ball! Get your tools and hit the road. You're fired!" I said to the guy.

Carl wasn't smiling anymore. In fact, he had the same worried look on his face that was there that morning.

Nobody ever did tell Carl he had been set up again. The man I had just fired was moving away. It was his last day anyhow, so we thought we'd use it to our advantage.

Got ya again, Carl.

STICK THAT IN YOUR PROP
AND SMOKE IT

I could hear the low slow rumble of his trolling motor long before I saw him coming around the rocky rise that sloped out into the lake. He stayed about twenty feet from shore and was getting close to me now. I could see the smirk of a smile on his face when he looked at me. "He must be able to see my fishing line," I thought. His boat was heading straight for it.

As his prop snagged my line cutting it in two he laughed, then continued on his way like nothing had happened. He had seen it all right. Up to now, I'd had a lake full of fish all to myself. I didn't need some jerk showing up and ruining it for me.

Showing him a hand gesture that didn't mean he was The Number One Fisherman, I reeled in my loose line and rigged it back up. Seeing me cast out, he turned his boat around and started toward me again. Was he crazy enough to do it a second time?

"I guess so," I thought as I heard the same laugh and my line went slack.

Now, I was mad! I walked to my pick-up and strapped on my holster that held a Blackhawk 357 Magnum. Grabbing my Surf Casting rod with a reel full of eighty-pound test braided nylon line, I was ready to put him to the test. "Hmm," I thought:

"This is a test of the
I Gotta Fish Network.
This is only a test.
In case of an emergency,
and if 80-lb. line don't stop you,
I'll be forced to kill your boat."

I casted out again, reeled in my slack, then opened the bail back up on my reel. I must admit I was surprised to see him coming back for a third pass. This time, I was smiling more than he was. When the prop caught on the line, it started peeling off my reel faster than anything I had ever hooked before. I don't think I want to catch the fish that can take line like a bass boat. The motor worked hard trying to keep running, but finally quit with a last dying cough. Whipping out my fillet knife, this time I cut my own line.

The jerk pulled his motor forward to check his prop. Looking down, he saw a large ball of fishing line where the propeller was suppose to be. Friction had melted some of the line to the shaft causing a cloud of steam that looked like smoke to rise up off the motor.

"Stick that in your prop and smoke it," I said happy with myself.

Standing up in his boat and shaking his fist he yelled, "YOU . . . !" then quickly sat back down when he noticed my right hand resting on the grip of my pistol.

The last I saw of him, he was drifting across the lake still trying to cut all the line off his prop. I never would have shot him, unless my life depended on it, but he didn't know that.

I'd have killed that boat in a second, though, if the line hadn't stopped it. I probably should have, anyway.

The test was now complete. I returned myself to my regular fishing.

Great Globs of Cheese Puffs

One warm February day my brother-in-law, Ken, a friend, Carl, and myself went fishing on the Snake River below Swan Falls Dam. The weather had been unseasonably warm for about a week and it was nice to be getting out to the river again after months of cold winter weather. I always look forward to the year's first fishing trip, even if it is just for a few hours.

We had met at Ken's house that morning. Carl drove up and got out of his truck. Dropping the tailgate down to let out his big black Labrador dog, he said, "I hope you guys don't mind if I bring my dog?"

We loaded our stuff and Carl's dog in the back of Ken's truck and headed for Swan Falls. Ken had brought along a giant bag of cheese puffs to eat along the way. Carl opened the sliding window behind his head and handed his dog a cheese puff. After that, whenever Carl's dog wanted another cheese puff he would stick his head into the cab through the back window and start to drool.

In a short time, the back of the seat along with the backs of our necks were soaked with drool. Curious about the source of the flood, I began to observe Carl's dog. How could so much fluid come from one animal? The dog's mouth was open and his tongue was hanging out to one side. Two cheese puffs caused long, stringy, orange-tinted drool to hang from each side of the dog's jaw. Droplets of the liquid would roll down his tongue and drip off the end. Occasionally the dog would pause in his panting to lick his lips. The tongue not only rolled across the dog's lips, but covered the surrounding face as well. After making a complete circle around the face, it would recoil back into his mouth sending orange drops flying in multiple directions. Any of the projectiles that managed to miss hitting us would land on the dash or windshield.

Six cheese puffs made the drool no longer transparent, resulting in slimey stripes on the windshield as it oozed down toward the dash. After twelve cheese puffs, large orange globs were clinging to the dog's gums.

I was going to bring this to my companions' attention, but upon closer observation I realized they both looked just like the dog. It would be like saying to someone "Hey, you got something stuck in your teeth." It might offend someone to say things like that, and anyway, who cares if Carl gives his dog a few cheese

114

puffs.

We had spent the entire afternoon fishing without a single bite. I had been fishing downriver from Ken and Carl and had just started to make my way back to them when I came across a large orange pile. Stepping around the smelly steaming pile, I continued along my way. Carl's dog walked by me with his nose held up, sniffing the air. In a few seconds I looked back and the dog was gobbling up the orange, almost pudding like, pile.

A few hundred yards further up the river, I saw Ken sitting high up on the bank watching Carl fish down at the river's edge. Sitting down beside Ken, we could see Carl's dog running along the river bank. The dog ran up to Carl wagging his tail and his tongue. Carl bent down and put a hand on each side of the dog's head. Leaning forward he said, "Where you been boy?" while the dog licked his face.

Carl suddenly jerked away yelling at the dog, "Your breath smells like crap!" He looked at the dog in disgust. "And you have orange globs of stuff stuck to your gums!" Using his finger, Carl scraped some orange globs from the dog's gums. Smelling it, he realized it was no longer the cheese puffs the dog had eaten earlier.

Turning to look at Ken I said, "Carl doesn't look too good. Was that your pile of cheese puffs down by the river?"

"Only the parts I didn't need anymore," Ken answered while watching Carl with a puzzled look on his face.

"Carl's dog ate it," I told Ken. We looked at

each and busted up laughing. Carl didn't see any humor in what had just happened, so Ken and I kept laughing until we were sure we had laughed enough for him and his dog.

On the way home, we had eaten enough cheese puffs to get some good gum globs started when Carl held one up by the rear window. Putting his head through the opening the dog scarfed down the cheese puff, then rolled out his tongue to ask for more.

Anyway, who cares if Carl feeds his dog cheese puffs.

Politicians Should be Thrown Back

I have never known a fish that lied to me. I don't know anybody that has been lied to by a fish, either. The same thing cannot be said about politicians.

I have never known a politician who didn't lie to me, and I don't know anybody else that has not been lied to by a politician.

During elections, we voters are told by politician wannabes what "honest, upstanding citizens" they are. They say "I'm an ordinary person just like all of you, and if elected, I will do my best to fulfill all my promises to you, the voters." Then they "promise to" do this and "promise to" do that.

"Lies, all lies." They are not just like me. I

don't stand up and lie to the whole nation. It wouldn't do any good, anyway. Nobody ever listens to me.

I think if all the politicians were doing their best to fulfill promises, at least *one* politician could have fulfilled *one* promise by now. We've been waiting centuries . . . how long is it going to take?

Some states have started allowing voters to mail in their votes. This is easier than standing in lines at voting booths and has resulted in more people voting. I'm told this also saves a lot of taxpayers' money.

Politicians disburse taxpayers' money in two ways: they steal it and they waste it. The money that doesn't go into their own pockets, they either give to some country none of us taxpayers care about, or they pay relatives and friends to do some useless "important government job."

These people have excellent job security. Like the politician's job, the objective is to never get anything done. They are payed billions of taxpayers' dollars doing nothing at a job where nothing ever gets done. Why is it called "taxpayers' money?" The taxpayer never sees the money again once the politicians get their hands on it.

Our elected officials pass laws that supposedly make it legal to steal taxpayers' money. As a voter, I'm not allowed to vote on these laws because they know that even though I was stupid enough to help vote them into office, I'm not stupid enough to vote for any laws that let them steal more taxpayers' money for "political reasons." Each time they run out of money, they raise taxes . . . and I didn't vote for that, either.

I have an idea for a system to keep politicians honest. In our computer-age world, all politicians should be listed Online on the Internet with two voting columns beside their names. One column for voter approval of their performance in office, the other for disapproval. Once a week the politician would be evaluated and if, at any time, there was a majority disapproval the politician would be impeached and the last election's runner-up would take the office.

When I catch a fish I don't want to keep, I unhook it and throw it back. If it's hooked too deep and I can't unhook it without injury, I cut the line and then throw it back. The same thing would work with politicians . . . with some slight modification. If one is caught doing something the voters don't like, throw him back. If they're hooked too deep, rip their guts out through their mouths, and then throw them back.

I'm a farmer and I feel that all politicians could help farmers. I'd like to throw one back in each field I get ready to plant. Every time politicians open their mouths fertilizer comes out, and it seems to be an inexhaustible supply.

120

TAKE ME ALONG
FOR THE RIDE

Early this morning, I went outside and kicked Duke a few times before twisting and jerking one of the lumps that stuck out of the side of his neck. A few choice words of encouragement, two or three more kicks, and then reluctantly Duke turned over, passed a little gas, and puked out a cloud of morning breath that burned my nose and made my eyes water. It was nice to find Duke was the same as usual and would live through another day.

I wasn't being cruel in the way I awakened Duke. I was only doing what was necessary. Duke's gas peddle sticks on cold mornings and must be kicked instead of pumped to get it to work. The lump on the neck of his steering column with a key stabbed into it must be twisted hard in a clockwise direction, then jerked down and forward to make contact. Oozing from his other lump is a tangled blob of broken levers and electrical wires that, at one time, enabled Duke to do tricks like bend the neck of his steering column and tell you which way he was going to turn. One of them even forced him to go a certain speed, but now he's lucky he can go at all.

Nothing happened when I pushed Duke's heater and defrost levers to the "on" position. This wasn't surprising. Nothing ever does happen. Hammering my fist down on a small area on top of the dashboard I keep cleared of tools and spare parts just for this reason, I listened again for the heater fan to turn on.

Nothing happened. Again, not surprising; nothing ever does . . . but it makes me feel better. With the palm of my hand, I hit Duke hard in the face of his clock that's above the heater controls. Sensing my hostility, Duke turned his fan on.

Duke's clock always says it's 7:05. Probably because he don't care what time it is, so there is no sense changing it, and I agree with him. Duke and I are a lot alike. My wife has to kick me to get me started in the morning, too, and she also twists *something* that's not on my neck.

Anyway, it was about this time, 7:05, that Duke's back door opened. It was one of my boys.

"Are you taking me and James to the bus stop?" Adam asked.

"Duke is," I answered. "But I'll go along for the ride."

122

Adam moved some five-gallon buckets off the seat and got in. Moments later, James got in the front and we left.

We were sitting in Duke waiting for the bus when James looked down and said, "Something stinks."

"So what's new?" I said. "You're always stinking up the place."

"It wasn't me!" James yelled as he rose up in his seat looking down between his legs.

"It never is according to you," I replied. "You act like you need to go home and change your pants."

"I don't think it's James this time," Adam added. "He smells lots worse than that."

I had just caught wind of the stink when James said, "I think it's coming from under the dash."

"Smells like burning brush," I said while pulling on the hood release lever. Quickly, I jumped out of Duke and threw his hood open. A cloud of smoke rolled up past my head and I could see Duke was on fire. "Huh! Looks like one of those bird nests fell down against the exhaust manifold," I said. " Guess I better put it out since it's also on top the gas pump."

"How come those birds build nests on Duke's engine?" Adam asked.

"I don't know. Hand me that peanut can." I dipped some water from the canal a few yards away and poured it on the flames just as they were spreading to Duke's oil and crud-covered engine. Lucky for Duke he took me along for the ride.

"Good thing Duke's gas pump wasn't leaking," I told James. "Remember when you held a lighted match next to your leaking gas pump?"

"Yeah, I'll never do that again. You can burn the whole seat of your pants right out, not to mention what you might singe."

JURY DUTY

The letter was official looking and addressed to me. I thought "It most likely starts out with You May Be a Winner If...! I'll throw it away just like I do the ones that say You Have Already Been Pre-approved For $$$."

"You better open it," my wife said. "The return address is the County Courthouse."

"Someone is probably suing us or something like that," I said suspecting the worst. "Did you tell the neighbor it was me who shot his dog?"

"Which time? You've shot six of his dogs so far," she reminded me.

"Hey, it's not my fault he keeps getting a new dog. He should teach'em to stay home instead of letting'em come over here. That reminds me, pick up another case of bullets when you're in town. I smell trouble."

I opened the letter and found it to be a questionnaire about jury selection. If I didn't answer the questions "to the best of my ability" it said, and return it in no more than ten days, I would be fined ten thousand dollars and be thrown in jail for ten years. Each question had two little boxes marked "Yes" or "No" next to them with "Check The Appropriate Box" explaining what to do. So, I answered them all true or false.

Let's see if they can prove I was "able" to do any different. I'll probably end up serving more time in prison because of a questionnaire than someone who has committed murder.

I don't know what's wrong with people who sit on juries these days. If the murderer says he did it because he feared for his life or the gloves he was wearing at the time were too small, they find him innocent. My favorite excuse that lawyers use is "He was temporarily insane."

"I plead Temporary Insanity for my Client, Your Honor," the lawyer says to the judge. "He was insane when he killed them, but he's all better now and is sorry it happened."

Instead of sending the killer to a sanitarium for a few months to be released when some idiot gets tired of talking to him, just once I'd like to hear a judge say, "I agree. To murder someone you have to be insane. Bailiff . . . Hang him!" Then slam down his hammer and say, "Case Closed!" We need more Capital

Punishment for the really terrible crimes and for that we need more Hanging Judges. If we singled out a few of the most corrupt judges and let them swing by a rope, the rest of them would wise up.

Over-crowded prisons are a problem costing taxpayers billions of dollars a year. Non-violent criminals serve longer sentences than the violent ones. I say, let's fine the petty crooks more, turn them loose, and use the money to finance the prisons we already have. There is no reason for it to cost the taxpayers anything. We didn't commit the crime. If it doesn't generate enough money to run prisons like vacation resorts, then that's too bad. Why should law-abiding citizens have to pay for weight rooms, game rooms, swimming pools, cable television, and law suits filed by prisoners who don't get enough crunchy peanut butter for lunch? I say, let's chain them to a tree, feed them gruel, and let them sleep on the ground. That would put a stop to repeat criminals saying "I didn't care if I got caught again. Life on the inside is easier than on the outside, anyway." Paroling crooks early could be kept in check by holding whoever paroled them equally accountable for a repeat offender's crimes. They obviously liked each other so they should make good cell mates.

I haven't gotten any more letters. I don't think they want me for jury duty.

I SEE YOUR LIPS MOVE BUT I DON'T HEAR ANY WORDS

y wife has a problem. She's been talking to herself a lot lately. I think she's saying things about me, too, because every time I catch her moving her lips, she's looking at me.

When she first started showing signs of having this problem, I would question her about it by saying things like "Huh?" or "What?" Interrupting her conversation with herself only made her mad. Then, she would yell at me shouting things like "I want you to do this!" or, "I want you to do that!" without even taking into consideration what I wanted to do. I was very content laying on the couch watching television and waiting for her to get supper ready. At least, until she started barking orders.

Trying to be helpful, I decided to convince her it didn't matter to me if she talked to herself. By nodding my head in agreement now and then and occasionally saying "It was OK" or "All right" for a while, she began to show signs of improvement.

But lately, she has started imagining that I've actually been talking to her. She starts out by asking me why I didn't do something she had talked to herself about and then tries to put the blame on me by saying, "You nodded your head last night while we were discussing it, and you said 'All right.' Why did you agree with me if you weren't going to do it?"

Puzzled, I told her, "I don't know what you're talking about."

"And I suppose you're going to tell me you don't know anything about the money you said I could spend on the house? You said it was OK."

"Do we have some money I don't know about?"

"Not anymore," she replied. "You must have imagined it. The problem with you is you're getting so hard of hearing you don't hear half of what I say."

"What?" I asked without thinking, causing her to have a relapse.

"If you weren't so darned deaf, I wouldn't have to yell at you!" she screamed.

"Oh yeah," I thought. "Shows how much she knows."

I've got a new cure for her problem. I'm starting to be able to read lips. So, if she doesn't want me to hear what she's saying, she'd better not look at me when she talks to herself.

130

THEY DON'T PHONE SOLICIT
ME ANYMORE

The woman on the other end of the phone line said, "Hello, can I please speak to *Mr. Jim Schwartz*?"

"This is him," I said. I hate it when people call me *Mr. Jim Schwartz*. It means they want something and if they are polite, it usually means they want money.

"I'm authorized to offer you such a good deal you simply can't refuse it. Would you like to hear more?" she asked.

"No, I refuse," I said.

"But I haven't told you how good the deal is yet," she begged.

"If it's such a good deal, why don't you keep it for yourself?" I asked.

131

"It's only offered to our new customers for a limited time . . . let me explain. For a low 4.9% interest rate, you can have a Major Credit Card with no annual fee and a $7500.00 pre-approved line of credit. Now, would you like to hear more?"

"No, but please tell me more," I said just to show her I could be polite too.

"The 4.9% interest rate is good for the first six months after your card is issued, and then will be adjusted to our standard low rate," she explained.

"And what is your standard blood-sucking rate?" I asked very nicely.

"Sorry to have bothered you, Sir." (Click)

Darn, I thought to myself. I didn't even get to find out what today's blood-sucking interest rate is.

Long distance companies call me all the time telling me lies hoping to get me to switch over to their service. Each one claims to have the cheapest rates with special discounts for their valued customers. I don't have a problem with the valued customer part. I'm a customer and all the money I give them is their value. As far as special discounts, what's so special about 20% off a 25% higher price if I spend $25.00 or more every month? Evidently, to them, a special discount is the same as saying "We really aren't going to charge you a higher rate so long as you agree to spend more."

Telling me lies and then promising to keep them doesn't help, either. That's the same as saying "Now that I've lied to you once, I promise to lie to you again." All I have to do is pay them. I can get the same service for free when I listen to the politicians on the evening news.

They all lie. How can every one of them be cheaper than all the other ones? If it was true, after they batted it back and forth a few times, they'd be paying me to use the phone. I'd open what used to be my phone bill and find a check written out to me instead. A little note would say "If you'd like to earn more money, please call everyone you know." When that happens, I'll believe what they say.

Now, when they call I name one of their competitors and say, "I'm talking to them on the other line right now, you'll have to call back later." My *True Choice* was I didn't want to talk to any of them in the first place and if they didn't have their wires crossed, they'd know I didn't have *Call Waiting*.

If they think I'm going to reach out and touch my friends and family, they're mistaken. It sounds perverted and I won't do it even if they pay me a dime a minute.

YOU ARE WHAT YOU EAT

The pigs that lived in the pasture next to my Uncle Lewis and Aunt Mildred's house had a crappy attitude about life and there was never a kind grunt between them. When the arguments were over food at feeding time, the grunts turned from mean to downright impolite.

At the time, I was only nine years old and did not understand pig grunt very well. Later in life, while working on construction crews, I learned to speak it fluently and can now grunt with the best of them. It doesn't even seem to matter if they have two legs or four. I realize, now, that what I thought was impolite then was sometimes just plain vulgar.

In fact, on every construction crew, there was a guy everyone else called "the grunt." He was normally 'he youngest and least experienced man on the crew. His job was to do what was called, naturally, grunt work. Any job that was hard enough it required one to grunt in order to accomplish it was considered grunt work. A good grunt grunted all day long. He would soon learn to spend all his time between hard-work grunts grunting obscenities to everyone else on the crew who he thought was responsible for his having to grunt in the first place.

My Aunt and Uncle's house did not have a septic system. A four-inch pipe carried all the household wastes to the middle of the pig pasture creating a mud hole for the pigs to "bathe" in.

After carefully placing some brownies in the toilet for the pigs' dessert, I would flush it and run outside to watch them fight over it. Hearing gurgling sounds coming from the pipe in their mud hole, the pigs would race toward the noise knowing the first one there always got the prize. Squealing and biting they would fight each other all the way there, mixing in a grunt whenever possible. With mouth open and on the run, a pig would scoop up the brownie along with mud, water, and paper, swallowing it all in a single gulp and then grunt with satisfaction.

Because of my regularity, I was only good for one or two brownies a day and this was far from being enough to feed all the hungry pigs. Those pigs depended on people to feed them and since it was so much fun to do so, I figured I'd better try to please them.

The pigs liked my homemade brownies so well I thought maybe I could just eat more, resulting in more brownies, but that would take too much work. . . and too much time. Using the dried up horse apples in the corral would work just as well and there was an inexhaustible supply of them so long as my Uncle didn't stop baling hay. The pigs didn't seem to mind the change, either. They scarfed up everything that came out of the pipe. I would flush about twenty horse apples down at once, then watch the pigs bobbing for them in the muddy water.

The phrase "eating like a pig" has a different meaning to me than it does to most people. The next time you have a crappy attitude about life, remember it could be because of the ham sandwich you had for lunch. And if you think you don't have to worry because you're a vegetarian, it doesn't make any difference. All living things have to eat in order to survive and plants love pig manure.

People that know me are always saying I'm full of it. I agree with them. But then, aren't we all?

You are what you eat!

OINK!!

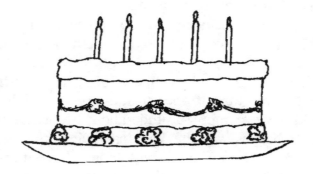

YOU CAN HAVE YOUR CAKE
AND EAT IT TOO

My family and I arrived early to what was called "A Pot Luck Dinner and Cake Auction." Each family there brought a cake decorated with a western theme to be sold to the highest bidder, the proceeds going to a good cause. They also brought something from home that they considered food to be contributed to the dinner. It was called a pot luck dinner because you were lucky if you knew what was in the pot. I knew what wasn't in the pots I looked into. (*Something Edible.*)

Leaning against a wall, I watched six boys enter the room carrying bags of ice. One boy had a scoop that he used to fill glasses. Spilling some ice on the table, he

139

stuck the scoop in his armpit to hold it while he picked the ice up with his other hand and put it into the glass. After wiping his wet hand off on his pants, he went back to using the scoop. Lacking scoops, the other boys used their hands and wiped them on their pants between filling glasses. One boy picked his nose and wiped that on the same part of his pants. Another one picked his nose and grabbed a handful of ice.

Seeing a man I knew walking toward me, I waved and said, "Hello."

"I hope you brought your money and your appetite," he said shaking my hand.

"Well, I have a little money, but no appetite."

"Looks like there's lots of good food here. Sure yer not hungry?" he asked.

"I'm hungry all right, but I lost my appetite watching those boys with the ice," I informed him. "I'm not going to drink anything, either." Then I told him everything I had witnessed the boys doing.

"That's no reason to pass up a free meal," he said with a shrug. "They're just being boys."

I told the man, "Reason enough for me. It's anybody's guess what's in that food."

"Some people will eat anything," I thought to myself. Pointing to a family carrying a big pot of chile to the table I said, "Look at those people all dressed up in their clean clothes. You can tell they're wearing their clean clothes because the snot isn't dry on their shirt sleeves, yet."

It made me wonder if the chile was runny, too. Or worse . . . maybe it was chunky. The youngest child sat

140

down and stared across the table at a cake. Something that looked like drool (but, I wasn't sure) was dripping from his chin as he repeatedly stuck the first two fingers of his right hand up his nose and into his mouth. "No," I decided. "This family's chile is definitely runny."

A little girl was having trouble choosing which kind of Jell-O she liked best. She moved from bowl to bowl sticking her finger into each one and licking the Jell-O off. Finally, she gave up and left her plate empty. She must have eaten her fill.

People with postnasal drip were hanging their heads over steaming pots and sniffing. Smiling they'd say, "Ummm," if they liked what they smelled or snort if they didn't. One boy could not keep spaghetti on a fork long enough to dish it onto his plate. Rubbing both sides of his nose (the inside and the outside) seemed to help him come up with a solution to his problem. He reached in the pot, grabbed a handful of spaghetti and slopped it onto his plate.

I don't eat other people's food, unless I'm sure they prepared it in a way that doesn't make me sick. People say I'm too picky, but I think they should keep their noses out of my picky business . . . and my food.

When I was asked to help eat one of the cakes, I refused saying, "No thanks, you can have your cake and eat it too."

142

Doctors Are A Waste Of Money

My wife wants me to write a story about why I won't fix my own breakfast. She says I'm lazy and will just lay on the couch while she does all the work. That is only half right. I will lay on the couch while she is fixing my breakfast, but being lazy is laying in bed to wait for it. I figure if she's going to get up and get dressed, then I will too.

Since I'm not lazy, I can't write a story about it. I don't know how to write fiction stories. Why would she ask me to write a fiction story when she tells me all the time that I don't know how to write! She amuses herself sometimes. I wish she'd let me do that.

When I was growing up, I got my underwear in pairs. Some of the poor kids only got one underwear, if they got any at all. It all started when I was somewhere between one and two years old. That's when I quit having daily accidents. My mother went right out and got me a pair of underwear because she knew that I was ready. Moms are really smart about stuff like that. Or, maybe it was just because she had three daughters before me to practice on. Either way, I still got my underwear and that is what was important.

My parents had two daughters after me. The last kid that is born in a family, I think, is the luckiest. By then, parents know what they are doing. There isn't any of that trial-and-error stuff that makes kids feel like guinea pigs being experimented on. Mom and Dad did pretty good, though, because all of us kids got a pair of underwear.

I know we did because I've seen all my sisters in their underwear. Did you know they have to wear twice as much as me? Three times as much if you count their top underwear as a pair. Girls are more expensive to raise than boys. At least twice as much, I think.

Like I said before, I saw all my sisters in their underwear. I told you again because I saw them more than once. You might think that I was being perverted, but that's just not true. I was only making sure that they did not get better or bigger underwear than I did.

This is one of the rules of nature. You never want a brother or sister to get anything better or bigger than you. After my sisters grew up, I noticed some of them were bigger than others. That's not being perverted either. I'm even bigger now that I am grown up. But, you will have to take my word for it because I am not going to show you my underwear.

A mother can be cruel. The first time you say to her "Mommy . . . potty" she picks you up, clamps you under her right arm and trots off to the bathroom. You think that this is what it's going to be like learning to ride a horse. She plops you down on a cold toilet seat with a hole so big it's scarey and your fingers automatically go under the edges of the seat.

There is something sticky under the edge of the seat, but that's okay. You're a kid and are always getting into sticky stuff. I mean . . . it's not like you knew any better. You didn't put it there. Just ask Mom.

All she cares about is that you go potty in the toilet with the cold seat. At least when you went in your pants it was warm. Sometimes even warm and soft. These days they have padded and heated toilet seats. Boy, doesn't that take you back to your childhood?

By now, your little knuckles are white where they bend under the sticky edge of the seat. Any minute you could fall in and drown. Mommy would say, "It's okay Honey. Just relax and go poo-poo in the potty. I won't let it swallow you when you fall in and drown."

I only needed one underwear during summer vacation from school. It didn't make sense to put a pair on. Then I would have one underwear on top of another one where my pants were supposed to be. I figured since I quit having accidents, why would I have to change my underwear? One underwear should be just fine. I did have to change my underwear when school started up again, though. My summer underwear had gotten so ratty I was getting tangled up in it. Guys have some parts that they just don't want tangled in their underwear. At least, my underwear hadn't gotten dirty. All the parts that would be dirty if I had an accident had broken off about midsummer.

Mom always bought me underwear in pairs. I would put one on and she would say, "Put this clean underwear in your pocket. You never know when you might have an accident and have to go to the hospital where someone will see your dirty underwear." Boy, if I ever have an accident in my underwear bad enough to put me in the hospital, I'm in real trouble.

Parents must have E.S.P. The older you get, the more things they told you when you were young seem to come true. One day I had two accidents. The first one was in my mom's garage when I ran a skill saw through my left hand. I cut bones and tendons, flipping flesh and

146

blood all over the floor. The saw did a really good job and my hand took a really big bandage. Big bandages are a guy thing. To other guys, a big bandage means you did a real good job of hurting yourself. No *guy* thinks twice about a band-aid.

The second accident was in my underwear. This is known as a chain reaction accident because it was caused by, and therefore connected to, the first accident. My wife drove me straight to the hospital emergency room. Doctors and nurses were waiting for us because Mom had called and said we were on our way. The hospital medical personnel took one look at my torn-to-shreds left hand and knew they would have to call in a specialist. Specialist is a scarey title. It means, in layman's talk, that they get paid lots of money. A nurse said, "What do you think, Doctor?"

The doctor pulled my clean underwear out of my pocket and said, "Good thing he brought these along. *Whew!* He needs a change of underwear!"

Picking up my medical chart, the doctor wrote . . . "Doctor Specialist. Diagnosis of Jim Schwartz. He needs his underwear changed . . . charge $500.00." Of course, you know what a doctor's writing is like. The pharmacist had to tell me what it said.

Just because Doctor Specialist has twelve years of medical school he thinks he can charge big sums of money. If I hadn't been unconscious, I could have made the same diagnosis and saved $500.00. I would have even changed my own underwear and saved another $500.00. Doctors are a waste of money.

I remember, now, what Mom really said. "Change

your underwear every day. You never know when you could be in an accident and end up in the hospital where someone will see them." If I had just remembered that correctly, I could have saved myself a lot of trouble . . . and a lot of money.

When I was a boy, my parents told me about a lot of things that would happen to me as I grew older. They sure were right. I hope my kids are smart enough to realize all the stuff I tell them is true and *will* happen to them . . . sooner or later.

Maybe one of them will become a doctor when they grow up so I can quit wasting money.

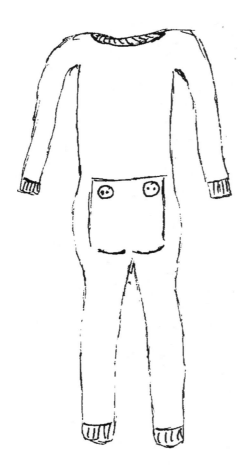

150

Zoie

Zoie is my dog. She is a pretty dog. I know that because people are always saying to me "Oh, what a pretty dog. What kind is she?"

I tell them, "She's a bad dog."

"No. I mean what kind of dog is she?"

"I told you. She's a bad dog."

There are only two kinds of dogs: Those that are bad and those that are not. The dogs that are not are called other dogs. That's because they always belong to other people.

Some of the other people have special names for their other dogs that they claim is the dog's breed. I don't believe them. All these other peoples' dogs came from other dogs and that just makes them all plain old other dogs. Most of these other people who have special names for their other dogs have lots of money. Some other people call their other dogs special names to make other people *think* they have lots of money. I, on the other hand, do not have lots of money. I don't have an other dog, either.

My dog likes me a lot. She lets me know this often by tasting me. She will be laying on the floor at the bottom of the stairs sound asleep. Sometimes I don't see her and almost step on her. She will jump up and taste me just a little bit on the foot. If I do step on her, she keeps tasting me most the way up the leg. That's when she likes me a lot.

Whenever anybody drives in our driveway, my dog will start barking and jumping and acting crazy. When I open the door, she will charge out towards the car. This will start all my kids' dogs to barking and going crazy. They will all chase the car until it stops, then run around it barking and growling. I will run out yelling *SHUT UP!* at them, but they can't hear me. They're all barking too loud. When I pick up a rock and threaten to hit my dog with it, she will stop and look at me. Her lips will part into a big smile showing off all her teeth that are permanently stained with my blood.

I know what she is thinking. " I'm young and I'm fast. You are old and slow. Go ahead . . . throw it. I'm hungry and I like you a lot."

If I was a dog I would be very old. I'm 42 now and that would be 294 in dog-years. I think my dog is 3, but I'm not sure because like most females, she won't tell her age. Anyway, in 12 years I will be 54 and she will be 15. That's 105 in dog-years. Then we'll see who is old and slow.

I like jerky. . . a lot. Red meat all looks and tastes the same when it is made into jerky. I think by the time I'm 54 I will like my dog . . . a lot.

154

THE NUT CRACKER MY
SWEET

If you were to ask me what I thought about a culture event, I'd have to say they serve a purpose. Culture is bacteria, something that can be deadly and is grown in a controlled environment. Later, the event that takes place is called decomposition.

Culture is very similar to Opera, a disease that has spread worldwide and is normally performed in a controlled environment. It kills me to listen to it, so it also stands to reason the event soon afterward is for me to decompose. I'd have to get an immunization shot to safely listen to the bellows of a fat lady with horns armed with a spear and wearing armor-plated underwear on the outside of her clothes.

Like Opera, another culture grown from bad bacteria is a disease known as Ballet. It also is found worldwide and is considered very contagious. It's spread by skinny little people dressed in skin-tight and sometimes see-through apparel. By using dance instead of words, they tell a story about how sick you're becoming. In some places of the world it's extremely contagious. They make you sick instantly by dancing in the nude. Fortunately for me, I don't ever expose myself to them.

Last night, there was a commercial on TV advertizing "The Cultural Event Of The Season." I wasn't paying very much attention to it because my wife, Martha, had just handed me a big bag of mixed nuts . . . the really good kinds that were still in their shells. Anyway, the big cultural event was about a little girl who got an ugly doll given to her at a party. Somebody breaks the doll and she forgets about it until later, when it comes to life. Promoters even thought they could sell tickets to people who wanted to go see such a thing. It would undoubtedly bore me to death.

Evidently thinking I was looking far too healthy for my own good, or possibly trying to do me in, Martha said, "You know, a little culture wouldn't do you any harm."

Feeling the need to change the subject I said, "Please pass THE NUT CRACKER my SWEET."

WANT A NEW BELT FOR CHRISTMAS?
BURN DOWN YOUR FORT

Every year I bale straw to sell in the fall. As soon as I get it in the stack, my boys are bugging me to let them build a fort in it.

"We'll only make a little one on one end," they say, forgetting that's the same lie they tell me every year.

I've been working hard for months with little rest and can use a vacation by now, so I take a week off work to waste my time explaining to them all the reasons why I don't want my straw stack messed up.

"But we'll only make a little one on one end," they tell me again thinking that I must have Altzhiemers. "Besides, you and Mom have been saying you would build us a fort out of old wood every year since we bought the farm."

"This old guilt-trip routine isn't going to work on me," I thought to myself. "How stupid do these boys think I am? I'll save myself a lot of work if I go ahead and let them waste a little bit of straw."

Quickly taking advantage of the opportunity I said, "OK, but just a little one and don't make a mess of the stack."

As the boys ran to the straw stack to begin construction, I realized that was the same way they got me to give in last year. Come to think of it, they say the same thing every year.

For days, the boys were telling me how cool their fort was becoming and when I finally decided to see for myself, I found they had taken the plans to last year's fort and doubled it. My straw stack had been transformed into a maze of tunnels and rooms covering three acres with a spiderweb of ropes and ladders leading in every direction. I'm sure glad they didn't build *their* version of a big fort.

For as many years as the boys have been building forts, I have been complaining to my wife, Martha, about the straw they waste and somehow she got the impression that I wanted her to do something about it. She came home from work one day and said, "It's time we built the boys that fort out of old wood like we promised."

"I didn't promise," I said. "I only told them I would build one someday. And someday ain't here yet."

"Yes it is," she said handing me a bag of hinges.

"I bought these for the doors. Now, get started!"

"I thought you said *we* were going to build it," I complained looking into the bag.

"WE ARE!" she shouted. "I bought the hinges, now *you* get it built. It can be their Christmas present."

Now that I knew what "WE" were going to do, I spent a couple weeks building it. The whole time, I grumbled to myself about wasting a week's vacation earlier arguing with the boys when they wanted a straw fort. When I had finally finished it, they said they thought it was really cool . . . until I told them no candles, lanterns, or matches were allowed in it.

"Why can't we have a lantern for light?" they asked.

"You can use a flashlight," I said.

I told them about the cool fort their grandpa built for me when I was their age. How me and two of my friends fell asleep with a candle burning and caught it on fire. By the time we woke up, the inside of the fort was burning and the top of my sleeping bag was on fire. Escaping a burning sleeping bag without being scorched is easy . . . if you're fast enough. It's surprising how fast you can be when the only alternative is to be toasted alive.

Later that night, I began to feel like I had jumped from the flaming bag into the flames. I could see a blazing reflection in my Dad's eyes. Although he had already put the fire out in the fort, he had rekindled a four-alarm inferno on the seat of my pants with his belt that I, for one, felt he had allowed to get completely out of control.

"So now, boys, guess what you will get for Christmas if you ever burn down your fort. It just so happens I always wear your size belt and will give it to you early . . . if I need to."

I GET MY HAIRS CUT AND EVERYBODY'S JEALOUS

Twice a year I get my hairs cut, whether they need it or not. It's supposed to happen in May and October, but sometimes my wife is too busy and it takes a month or two extra for her to get around to doing it. So if I start looking a little shaggy, it's plain to see it's all her fault.

My sister, Debi, told me once, "I've got four sisters and one brother. We're all the same except Jim's got more hair." She's just jealous.

People are always saying to me, after my wife gives me a shearing, "You got a hair cut." Don't they think I already know that? I'm quick to correct them and point out I got *all* my hairs cut. They really should try to be more observant. At least it's evident they're paying attention enough to see how good-looking I am because they say things like "You clean up real nice," and "When those whiskers are trimmed, you're a lot more handsome. Why don't you shave them all off so we can see how good looking you really are?"

I've never been one to brag, but since they asked I go ahead and tell them why I don't. I got all my hairs cut and shaved all my whiskers off once and it got me into a lot of trouble. Women couldn't look at me without saying how cute I was. Then, they would start babbling things nobody understood and fighting each other just to hold me. It seemed no female could keep her hands off me. This made my wife very jealous so I grew the whiskers back just to keep her happy. I'm always doing nice things like that for Martha, but she has a funny way of showing her appreciation. She thinks I'm mistaken and haven't shaved in so long that I'm remembering when I was a baby without any whiskers. She tells me women always think babies are cute and want to hold them. She can come up with the strangest excuses to hide her jealousies.

An old neighbor lady told me, one time, that she absolutely hated hair on men's faces and I was handsome enough I didn't have to hide behind a bunch of whiskers. Of course, I agreed with her and explained it was for my own protection. She gave me a thoughtful look as I told her that if I didn't hide my good looks, every woman in the country would be after me. I could tell by the expression on her face it hurt her just to think about what I had said. She must have been visualizing me, *in all my handsomeness*, being trampled by a herd of out-of-control women. Finally, she smiled and tried to sound serious when she said, "Well, it works for me."

She's just jealous because all her whiskers are grey.

Note the similarities in appearance of the author in this picture to the drawing of his Uncle Grog. No, Grog was not drawn to look like the author. He was drawn because, millions of years ago, cameras were scarce.

Very strict guidelines were followed in creating this book to protect its authenticity. A photograph of Uncle Grog might arouse some suspicion, prompting readers to think it was a fake. That's why I didn't use it.

FUR SIGHTED AND FUZZY FACED

My wife's normal talking voice has dropped to less than a soft whisper because the noise hurts her ears. "Turn that TV down!" she yells at me. "It hurts my ears."

"That's because you're yelling at me again," I say. She's not happy until I turn it down so low I'm not able to hear it.

"If I had my way, we wouldn't even have a TV," she adds. "And, I don't know why you bother to watch the old thing anyway. You can't hardly see it."

"That's because the picture is all fuzzy," I say. "I think we should get a new one. Maybe one of those big screen types."

Stepping close to me, she screams, "We are not getting a new TV!" so loud that the little hangy-down wanger at the back of her mouth stretches out in front of her teeth and makes her look like she has two tongues.

The only place I had ever seen that happen before was on cartoons. Man, would it hurt if her mouth slammed shut before that wanger recoiled!

Believing that she "spoke with forked tongue" and not wanting to irritate her, I quietly said, "Yes dear."

Quick to realize that it would be in my best interest to change the subject, I pointed out to her how fuzzy her face was getting.

"I didn't notice it so much when you were in the other room," I said. "But, up close it kind of looks like a fur coat."

"I'd tell you to take my truck and go get some glasses, but it won't do any good until you check your poor hearing," she whispered.

"I don't know if your glasses are in the truck, or not, and I checked the power steering yesterday," I answered softly so I wouldn't hurt her ears. She stared at me a moment and then shook her head as she walked away to see if she could find her glasses.

My youngest son, Adam, who had been listening said, "Mom has her glasses on Dad. Didn't you see them?"

"If she has them on, then how come she's looking for them?" I asked, just a little confused, and then noticed how fuzzy Adam's face was getting. "You're sure growing up fast. How old are you now?"

"Ten, almost eleven," he answered.

"Your mother doesn't listen to me anymore. Go ask her to teach you how to shave."

My Way

Have you ever been criticised for doing something wrong? It really makes me mad and I usually correct the air-headed criticiser on the spot.

Someone says that you speeled that rong. My kids tell me that a lot. You wood think theyed know better by now. Even my oldest son, James, has been known on more occassions then he can count, to say "You spelled that wrong." Instantly, I think of *Bull Stuff* and very polightly say, "No. I didn't."

One time I spelled potato. Actually, I've spelled it more than once, but this particular time I spelled potato was because James asked me to. Then, he had the nerve to tell me there was no "e" on the end of potato. Well, I had two words to think about that, but I said: "Look at it. Anybody that knows their ABC's could see there was an "e" on the end." I pay hundreds of dollars in school taxes and he can't even learn when there is an "e" on the end of a word. What a waist of money. He continues to insist that I spelled it wrong and then I think those two words again.

I don't like people telling me, "You should start a new paragraph here." It makes me think about taking a sharp pencle and tattooing a new pairagraf esspecially for them right where they will be reminded of it every time they sit down to right about something. Instead, I tell them I'm rightin' this and I'll put the darn pairagraf wherever I want. What are they gonna do, call the English Police? Some people get so upset because you didn't use enough pairagrafs . . . according to them.

I can see it all now. I'm standing trial for leaving out a pairagraf or two on a page I wrote. A jury of English teachers finds me guilty. (I never did care much for English teachers when I was going to school and now I know why.) One day, while waisting away a life sentence in prison, this guy says to me, "Hey, I'm getting out tomorrow."

I say, "Hey, that's great! How long you been in for?"

"Six months," he replies.

"Six months! What kind of a rap did they pin on you?"

"Murder. I killed two people. I would have gotten the maximum sentence, except they spelled potato with an "e" on the end. Besides, I know a guy on the

170

parole board and he substitutes as an English teacher. What are you in for?"

"Oh, I wasted some geek for not using enough pairagrafs."

No point in telling this guy that I was framed for not using enough pairagrafs myself. I try not to lie, but there was no sence in saying something that might set him off. Some people get set off so easy nowadays.

Anyway, I had just been thinking of two words when James told me, again, I had mispelled a word. I don't understand why I am always having to explain myself. People nowdays just seem to always want to argue . . . even if there rong. It seems I'm always having to prove I'm rite. Fortunatly that's easy for me to do because of a rule of conduckt that I always follow: "Don't do anything rong and I will always be rite." This rule is so simple its funny that I'm the only living human that can follow it flawlessy.

So, I asked James, "Did you not ask me how I spell potato?"

"Yes, and you spelled it wrong."

There's those two words again. My wife says it's wrong to think those words. I had to explain to her that she's wrong. Those two words best sum up exactly how I feel about people who are not smart enough to realize I'm right.

"James, you asked me how I spell potato and I spelled it the way I always spell it unless I happen to leave the "e" off. And if I do leave the "e" off next time I spell potato, then that's the way I spell it. Either way you read it you think of two words: butter or gravey. Do you understand what I'm talking about?"

If'n ya cain't reed and unnerstan whot I'm riting than ya is to stewpid ta be readin this here stuff. An if'n yer two stewpid too reed and unnerstand this, than ya need yer own inglish tootor ta teach ya one-on-one cuz ya shur don't wont no one else ta no how stewpid ya is.

Thare -- now. I'm right again! And, if you have anything critikill to say about my punk-chuation, I got five words for you:

I Don't Like English Teachers.

JUST ASK ME, I'LL TELL YA

First, I would like to thank you for purchasing my book. THANK YOU!

I hope you enjoyed it and would very much like to hear from you. If you want to tell me your opinion of the book or have any questions or comments, you can write to me at this address:

Jim Schwartz
3500 Elmore Rd.
Parma, Idaho 83660

I have more opinions than I need and don't mind giving some of them away.

ABOUT THE AUTHOR

As an infant, Jim sat in his high chair making ditches and dams in his mashed potatoes so he could irrigate the green vegetabbles on his plate with gravey. Shortly after his first day of school, he decided he would move away to live off the land as a bachelor hermit and teach his kids to do the same.

I feel proud that my son is one of those rare individuals who has managed to realize a childhood dream. He lives off the land outside Parma, Idaho . . . with his wife and their kids. He is at peace with himself and most of the world around him.

Helen, mom #1

Brother?! Why didn't someone tell me I had a brother? I thought that funny little creature was the troll Grandpa said lived in his cellar.

Karren, sister #1

I often wished for a different big brother . . . anyone would do as long as he slept in the house where he belonged, had no desire to smother me with filthy socks and derived no pleasure from pinning me to the floor and forcing me to eat canned dog food. Cheap canned dog food!

Bobbi, sister #4

Oh boy, where do I begin . . . being the youngest daughter in the Schwartz clan, I've escaped most of the horror that was dished out by Jim. I do remember a few times when I was asked to pull his finger. You'd think that the older I get, I would learn to take a little more precaution with Jim. Like when he says, "Hey, you wanna go for a ride in Duke?" or "You wanna see my stitches?"

Debi, sister #5

Nothing Jim does anymore surprises me. Do you ever wonder if there are, in fact, other civilizations out there? How about if any of them are secretly living here on Earth among us??. . .

Jim was, like, born way too late . . . this is not his century.

Judie, sister #3

Jim Who???

Jim Who was only thirteen when I got married and moved away from home. Up to that time, he had been a relatively insignificant irritant in my life . . . an 'only brother' who contributed little more to the family than skidmarks in the laundry load. (And probably still does, given his ongoing prideful, personal commitment to promoting Flatulence as an Olympic sport.)

Sandee, sister #2

—————·•●••—————

Have you ever seen what a Troll's sister looks like? It's no wonder Grandpa hid me in the cellar.

I didn't sleep in the house because my older sisters kicked me out. If they didn't pull my finger, I did it myself.

Dad bought cheap dog food because it was . . . well . . . cheaper, and he got real mad if it was wasted. The dog wouldn't eat it, so I fed it to my sister. I was only being kind to animals. That way the dog didn't get in trouble. Besides, my socks would have been too hard for her to swallow.

THERE ARE other civilizations out there and I've got a surprise for you. I've been secretly living here on Earth for centuries.

Who's Sandee??? I'd like to flatter her by saying something Flatulent.

Jim, brother #1

Hushed Puppy Jerky

1 smoldering fire   1 dog (well aged)

Season to taste
Serve to other people